OCCUPIED A

The Story of Friern Barnet Library

Edited by

Rosie Canning

London
2018

The Greenacre Project
32 Long Lane
London N3 2PU

ISBN: 9780956991430

A catalogue record for this book is available from the British Library

Printed in Great Britain

OCCUPIED AND OPENED

The Story of Friern Barnet Library

CONTENTS

INTRODUCTION

RICHARD STEIN
Solicitor and Partner, Leigh Day

I feel extremely honoured to have been asked to write an introduction to this book about recent events around Friern Barnet Library which describes the wonderful way that this really important resource was saved by the community standing up and standing together against all the odds.

It is essential to recognise the extremely important historical role that protest has played in Britain throughout the centuries in protecting and advancing progressive interests against the reactionary forces protected by the state. From the peasants' revolt through the chartists to the women's suffrage movement and the anti-poll tax campaign, and now the Occupy Movement, protest (including direct action) has always played an integral part in delivering any advances in the rights and interests of ordinary people. The campaign to save Friern Barnet Library has shown that this essential element of British society is still alive. Although in recent times it often looks to be dead, it is only dormant, and it can be roused. When it is, as this book shows, it can be extremely powerful. It also demonstrates graphically that people power has many elements and requires alliances of many kinds of people with different experiences to work together and to take a variety of actions to be successful.

Public libraries are symbolically very important in our society. They were one of the early manifestations of public service provision paid for out of the rates and delivered by elected local councils. The first Public Libraries Bill was introduced in the House of Commons in 1849 and immediately faced resistance from Conservatives, many of whom were of the mind that "people have too much knowledge already: it was much easier to manage them twenty-five years ago; the more education people get the more difficult they are to manage". The Carnegie Trust UK, whose name is intimately associated with hundreds of public library buildings throughout the UK, notes that in 1883, when the first

9

Carnegie library was opened in Dunfermline, only 23% of the British population had access to a public library service.

As public libraries spread through the country they provided a local cultural resource for the whole community, rich and poor. The library is historically one of the most important and effective ways of providing education and learning to people who could not otherwise access it. The philosophy underpinning the donation of public library buildings by the Carnegie Trust was that local authorities should provide staff and resources and they would become places where people could understand that even if they could not afford to buy books, they could read them. They became places for poor people and old people and lonely people who would go to read a newspaper or a book or just to spend time in the company of others. Unfortunately, in some circles libraries are now no longer so popular. We can buy books from Amazon, read them in the privacy of our homes or use our computers to find out what we need from the internet, and so some feel that libraries are no longer needed.

As a result, many of those responsible for allocating the community's resources see them as an easy target for cuts. It is true that libraries no longer serve exactly the same function as they did in the past; however, there's still a great need for professional librarians in libraries. The local library is a hugely important local resource which galvanises people in many ways.

Barnet Council was not alone in focusing on libraries as easy targets for cuts following recent massive reductions in local government funding. There have been several other campaigns to save libraries around the country, including a very lively campaign in neighbouring Brent. However, what singles out the Friern Barnet library campaign for me was the amazing energy, imagination and creativity with which the campaigning resources were brought to bear to force Barnet Council to change its plans.

The Council's policy to reduce Barnet's library provision culminated in the decision to close Friern Barnet library in April 2012. The response of the community to that decision was extraordinary. I don't think the Council has recovered from the shock – even now!

What made the campaign so powerful was the wonderful way in which so many diverse and different groups and individuals from so many different walks of life came together and found a way of collaborating to achieve a common aim. That being said, I don't think we should gloss over how difficult this was. I'm sure at first many of the individuals and groups looked at each other and had huge doubts about how and indeed whether, they could collaborate. Nevertheless, through the experience of talking and working together an exceptional level of cooperation was brought about. Ultimately, it was precisely this extraordinary alliance of organisations and people with a shared objective, who would normally have been expected to have been impossible to unite, which was so powerful that it drove all of the opposition away before it.

The main elements of the campaign comprised local political and community organisations, some of which had already expressed concerns at the general direction the Tory council was taking. Many local people who had never campaigned before initially thought that they could petition the Council and that the Council would listen and not close their library. They soon learned that, despite their protests to local councillors and officers, the Council were determined to close the library regardless. They were told that it was not practical, not affordable – indeed impossible for the library to remain open. The community felt helpless, not because they considered there was any legitimacy in the Council's position, but because they did not think there was any way they could change the Council's mind.

It seems to me from outside that the galvanising factor for the whole campaign was the arrival of Phoenix and the others from the Occupy Movement. Their huge experience of taking these forms of direct action all over the country to support and articulate popular community interests, along with their energy, ideas and enthusiasm seemed to give the campaign a massive confidence boost.

Before the arrival of the occupiers many local people, despite their anger about the stance of their local council, would probably not have wanted to have anything to do with these most unlikely of allies. They would have heard about other actions taken by people like them, communicated through the media, usually in derogatory terms, and would never have imagined themselves in alliance with 'squatters'. However, in working together to save the library, the Occupy Group and the local community soon forged strong links and started collaborating. Had it not been for this alliance then I think it's fair to say that the chances of achieving the success celebrated in this book would have been extremely slim.

The most important thing about involving such disparate people from different backgrounds is the range of experience, skill and ability that they were able to bring to bear on the situation. Clearly their opponents at Barnet Council were in an extremely powerful position. They had the support of the government and all of the establishment, and all the power, resources and authority which that brings. In the end, they were defeated by the way that the broad alliance of different individuals, groups and interests who wanted to keep Friern Barnet library alive were able to win the argument. It is stunning to look at a wonderful variety of different campaigning tools employed by the campaigners. They arranged leaflets, posters, petitions, meetings, demonstrations, and pop-up libraries. They occupied the library - first for few hours and then for five months! They reactivated it and showed how a library run by the community for the community could function. Ten thousand books were donated by the local community so that the empty shelves of the library were filled within no time. They planned and facilitated a huge range of events and activities in the library. Yoga and Pilates classes, French and Chemistry lessons, creative writing workshops all took place. Music became integral to the running of the library where bands such as Dijitalis, The Hamptons and Blues of Cain performed, and wonderful cabaret evenings were organised with poets, singers, troubadours and activists. There were conferences – 'Love Story Past and Present' with slide shows, presentations and local and national library campaigners, and endless discussions. A particular highlight was the visit from Will Self. It is not surprising that both local and national media began to take an interest in this wonderful demonstration of how a community could, if it turned its mind to it, run its own facility brilliantly.

I know that this idea of communities running their own facilities is not without difficulty. The government's Big Society initiative is seen by many as a cynical way of undermining the services provided by local authorities and instead replacing them with volunteer services on the cheap. Our communities are particularly proud of the tradition of voluntary participation in community activities. However, the attempt to move libraries from being organisations at least led by professionals to much more informal organisations without paid staff is a very worrying one.

The part that the law played in saving Friern Barnet Library from closure was a very significant one. This was not because we had any long-term victories in court. We ultimately lost the hearing in December 2012 at Barnet County Court and the Council capitulated before we were able to see what the Court of Appeal would have said. Clearly in cases such as this one, the campaigners had no real choice about whether to go to court. They did not start the legal action in a way they do when campaigners bring a judicial review of a decision by government, a council, or, say an NHS body. Here the Council used the law to issue proceedings in Barnet County Court to recover possession of the library. Therefore, the protesters were put in a position where they could either hand the library back or go to court to resist.

Again, the huge experience of Phoenix and the other Occupy campaigners in court proceedings like this was a huge bonus. I suspect that, had the occupation only been organised by the local community, it would have ended at that point. However, in fighting the Council in court Reema Patel played a massive role as the defendants' 'McKenzie friend'. She did a wonderful job, using all of her newly developing legal skills to assist the campaigners. It must have been a terrifying experience for her that she will never forget! Even though the court hearing on 10 October 2012 was not formally 'a victory', in the history of the campaign it was a hugely important date. Had the Council obtained possession in the middle of October 2012, it is extremely unlikely that Friern Barnet Library would be open now. It would have been closed, boarded up and sold. Again, I'm certain that the large number of campaigners obviously representing all parts of the community, who filled the court room to bursting and even overflowed into the lobby for the hearing, had a substantial impact on the way that the judge dealt with the case. The judge decided to delay the full hearing of the case until the occupiers had had an opportunity to marshal their arguments and obtain legal advice. That gave the campaign an extra two months to build not only their legal case but also their campaigning strength to fight the Council.

We at Leigh Day were then extremely pleased to be invited to be involved in the case on behalf of the defendants who had been named in the possession proceedings. With the campaigners we all had to work extremely hard to prepare the case for the hearing at very short notice in December. We had some memorable meetings when I particularly enjoyed and marvelled at the wide range and backgrounds of the people at the meeting representing different parts of the community and other partner organisations as well as Phoenix and others from the Occupy movement. It was immediately apparent to me that there was a huge amount of tolerance, respect and mutual understanding which made it a wonderful group of people to work with in promoting the justice of their case.

Ugo Hayter from my office, a hardened campaigner turned lawyer, played a major part in working on the case along with Reema Patel and our barrister Sarah Sackman. For me as a lawyer there is nothing better than to be able to work with groups like the Save Friern Barnet Library Campaign. It allows me to reactivate all of my past experience as a community and political activist and campaigner as well as a local councillor. I think we all worked together extremely well and prepared what we thought was a winning case for the hearing on the 17th of December 2012. Sarah Sackman presented the case extremely well and I think the judge was in some difficulty justifying her decision not to find in our favour. However, her judgment was a surprise and a huge disappointment to us all.

We did not give up and we immediately launched an appeal in the Court of Appeal. At this time, although the Council had won the battle in court, they were losing so overwhelmingly in the library, in the community and in the local and national media that they were forced into agreeing to allow the library to be reopened as a community facility. The legal process played a major part in holding things up for two to three months while arrangements were put in place to safeguard the library's future. It also kept another spotlight on the negative approach the Council was taking, how unacceptable it was and how weak its justification for closing down and selling off the library.

The councillors and officers in Barnet who had to make such a massive climb down will, I am sure, never forget the experience. I'm afraid that it is too easy for those in positions of power and authority to forget the reason why they've been elected or the reason why they are paid a salary by the public to deliver services. Unfortunately, I think when they become remote from the people, they are there to serve, they begin to believe their own rhetoric much too easily. I hope that this experience will mean that in Barnet, when the Council carries out its functions in future, councillors and officers will think much more carefully about the views and wishes of their masters in the community and the potential consequences if they ignore them! I'm sure all the people who were involved in the campaign and have celebrated keeping the library open will, in future and when the need arises, be ready to engage again in direct action to protect their community and its interests.

A HALLOWED PLACE

ROSIE CANNING

Friern Barnet Library is a lovely building. Predominantly red brick, it was built in 1934 in a mock Tudor style. There are large leaded windows all around which flood the interior with light from all angles giving the feel of a large art studio. Inside there are oak fitted bookshelves, panelled doors, and wood block floor. This building, its books, activities, and people have lain at the heart of Friern Barnet community life for over eighty years.

Fifty-five years ago, when I was five years old, I used to walk alone to my local library in Childs Hill. I spent many happy hours sitting cross-legged on the wooden floor discovering the magical world of books that took me on journeys to make-believe lands. As I grew older, I progressed from fairy stories to teenage adventures and then to murder mysteries, romance, horror and literary fiction. Although I loved *Lord of the Rings* and the Narnia adventures, I wasn't keen on Science Fiction. That lasted until I went to university and discovered the intellectual worlds of Arthur C. Clarke, Isaac Asimov and others. What I also remember about my childhood visits to the library, was the experience of discovering what I thought were secrets on the shelves – books that had been accidentally left behind and should really have been removed. I loved peeping into other people's lives.

I never minded the peace of the library; in fact, I hoped library staff would tell those noisy people to be quiet: it was the hallowed space, the wardrobe into other lands, a place to study, to read, to write – a place of safety. Libraries were my escape from a sometimes harsh world. Books were my medicine. They made me well. They set me free and let me know that there were other realities that transcended my own and they gave me hope.

My relationship with libraries has continued all my life. From eight years old, I used Sutton Road library as we called it then (South Friern now) and whilst at secondary school, Friern Barnet Library became my local. When some years ago, I got a job working for Middlesex

University in the library at Trent Park, I was in heaven. I also travelled to other campuses, because in those days Middlesex University had lots of sites and lots of libraries. Like many other institutions they have closed all their libraries bar one. This trend, like falling dominoes, seems unstoppable. It is now predicted that by 2020, 1,000 libraries will have closed in the United Kingdom.

When I hear of libraries closing and in particular public libraries, as in the case of Friern Barnet, I can't help thinking of all the other children who, like myself, never had any books at home and who may need their library as a haven.

In the summer of 2011, I wrote an article entitled, 'The Book People', which appeared in our local community magazine, *The Greenacre Times*. In this article I looked at the history of libraries in general and more specifically at the libraries in the London Borough of Barnet and the proposed cuts which had put two of them under threat of closure. The article ended by reporting that more than 5,000 Barnet residents had signed petitions against these proposed closures.

Since the original article appeared, three of our public libraries have been closed: Totteridge, Hampstead Garden Suburb and Friern Barnet. On the 4th April 2012, Barnet Councillors voted to close Friern Barnet Library forthwith. Closure was set for the following day at 5pm but council officials arrived unexpectedly at lunchtime. They tried to close the building early to avoid public protest which was rumoured to be taking place at 4pm. This plan backfired on them for such was the feeling amongst the public that they staged a spontaneous sit-in. People who had never protested in their life before, refused to leave and stayed put for several hours before the building could be closed and sealed that evening.

However, the story of Friern Barnet Library didn't end there, what happened next is the stuff of fiction. I could never have imagined the maelstrom of events, the explosion of spontaneous happenings that changed the course of local history and temporarily took over my life in the latter part of 2012.

THE PEOPLE'S LIBRARY

FROM ROGER TICHBORNE'S BLOG:
99% is ....The Barnet Eye

When a local community loses its heart, it's inevitable that it will die. Local communities can be built around many things; a church, a pub, a cricket club. In Friern Barnet, it is the local library which is the focus of the community. It is situated on a village green, and was set up in the 1930's with a loan from the Carnegie Trust. Sadly, for the residents of Barnet, we have a local authority which places no value on community and the hubs which nurture it.

Shortly after the 2010 council elections, Barnet Council announced that it was holding a strategic library review. Rather alarmingly the cabinet member responsible, Robert Rams, announced that people could "get books from Tescos". He also suggested that maybe people could read books in Starbucks. I organised a petition to keep all of our local libraries open. Conservative councillors were lobbied at their surgeries. We also made sure that everyone got the message that they would lose their library if they didn't take action. Soon we had collected the 7,000 signatures required to compel a debate.

Robert Rams got the message. He realised that many of the libraries were in Tory wards and that it could cost them dear if they carried out their plans. In March 2011, when the strategic library review was presented, only two libraries were targeted for closure. One was Friern Library, the other was in Hampstead Garden Suburb. The HGS library was in a strong Tory ward, and soon a deal had been done to keep it open as a community library with support from the council. Friern, being a Labour ward, received no such treatment. Although the council pretended to be interested in community plans, they had no intention of doing anything other than selling the building and pocketing the cash. Community groups were strung along for months. This was purely to avoid a legal challenge. Once the period for consultation passed, the library was cruelly shut with only 24 hours notice. People did not even have the chance to return books. A small occupation of the building was staged on April 5th, but after several hours people left and the library was shut.

I was contacted by Councillor Kate Salinger who told me that she attended the library at 3pm earlier that day to return some books before it closed. On arrival she was greeted by a large group of protestors, who complained about the withdrawal of toilet facilities. She immediately called Richard Cornelius who arranged for the facilities to be made available to protestors.

Kate assures me that Richard Cornelius is a decent guy and was not aware of the toilet ban when she called him. Let's hope that all parties have learned something from the incident.

Dear Councillor Cornelius   *5th April 2012*

I am sending you this open letter, because I am shocked and outraged at the treatment of local residents at Friern Library on Thursday 5th April. As you are no doubt aware, a group of local residents, upset by the withdrawal of library provision, gathered to stage a sit in at the library. Although Barnet Council had stated that the library would shut at 4pm, it was closed considerably earlier.

A group of 15 people remained in the library until approximately 6pm. It appears that officials working for Barnet Council refused to allow the group, some of whom were elderly, to use the toilet facilities in the library. As someone who suffers from a medical condition, which requires relatively frequent trips to the lavatory, I can only recoil in horror at this refusal to provide a basic human right. In my dealings with you, I have formed the opinion that you are a decent and honest fellow. I cannot believe that you would wish to subject residents who are clearly concerned about their community, to the indignity of using a bucket in a public place, to go to the toilet...
Regards, Roger Tichborne

 Mrs Angry said...
I think it is clearly now a pisspot, rather than tinpot dictatorship. It really does stagger belief that the senior officers involved forced residents to use a wastepaper bin to pee in: as you say the group included elderly people, but also I believe there was at least one child present. Cllr Kate Salinger told me herself that she had had to go and order the officers to allow residents to use the loo: just incredible, and yet another spectacular PR gaffe by Barnet Council. As the head of Communications & PR was present at the sit in - I saw

18

him outside at one point - what does it say about his judgement that he allowed this to occur?

I immediately announced, in my blog "The Barnet Eye", that we would hold a 'people's library' on the village green next to the library on the following Saturday. Hundreds of people turned up and a carnival atmosphere ensued. People brought tea, cakes and posters in addition to books. They also brought gazebos. The Save Friern Library campaign took over the running of the people's library and the event was staged every week throughout April and May. We even got a visit from the BBC's One Show!

THE DOORMAN

MR GREENACRES

Last summer as August turned to September, it was still fine and balmy and as yet there was not a sign of autumn in the air. On September the 5th 2012, all thoughts of summer dreaming and good things to come were rudely interrupted by the beating of jungle drums. The wires were humming; fragmented information was beginning to filter through the grapevine – "THERE ARE PEOPLE IN FRIERN BARNET LIBRARY." Whatever could this mean? Clarification was immediately sought and within a short space of time, we had received the incredible piece of news that the people in the library were from the Occupy Movement - they were squatters. By this time dusk was falling and I felt it was better to investigate in daylight, in person.

The following day, just after midday, I headed for Friern Barnet Library. At this point the news seemed incredible and something I dare not believe until I saw it with my own eyes. As I approached the library, all was quiet; there was no sign of occupation; no flags, or banners, or people. And no one was on the adjoining green. I went up to a front window and peered through. The building was dark and empty. So it had been too good to be true, the building was unoccupied. Undeterred, I went round to the back gate, hoisted myself up and peered over. I saw one fellow in the small courtyard, who opened the gate. I introduced myself and he told me his name was Dave Skipper. I heard a noise above my head and looked up to find another friendly face poking out of an open window, some ten feet above ground level. This turned out to be John Byrne, who had slept there the previous night. He told me that a couple of others had slept there too but had found it unsuitable and moved on. As yet no doors were open. The only access and ingress was through the small high-level window that John had poked his head out of. Dave said he couldn't get through the window. And when I looked up I agreed, I wouldn't attempt it either, it was too small and too high.

Morale seemed to be low, Dave didn't seem too keen on staying and

John was on his own in the building. I quickly realised that as yet this was no storming of the Bastille, no D-Day invasion. The beachhead had not been secured and in fact this occupation might be in danger of fizzling out altogether. Without even stopping to think, I knew what had to be done. I knew it instinctively and intuitively and I knew it was right. I had to get this building open and be quick about it.

Lady Luck smiled on us for John revealed that the keys to all the doors were inside the building. The problem was that the rear doors had been boarded up and extra locks had been added to the exterior of the front doors. I rushed off to get tools and when I returned we set about removing the boarding from the rear door.

The rear door and doorframe are original features. The door is a charming multi-panelled affair set in a sturdy frame and both are of oak. In a callous act of wanton barbarism, the council had ordered someone to screw plywood across the outside of this door, hardly a fitting way to treat a heritage building. The ply was secured every ten inches or so with 2½" screws. The trouble was that some of these screws were *very* tight and we ran the risk that unless we were very careful, we would chew the heads up in trying to undo them. I adopted a special technique for this task. I selected a brand new 15" screwdriver for maximum purchase and leverage, inserted the tip into the screw head and pressed my breastbone against the handle. I then grasped the handle with both hands and, with my forearms acting like the blades of a propeller, turned very slowly while pushing very hard.

On some stubborn screws, I had to get John and Dave to push my shoulder blades towards the door for extra purchase. It was in the midst of these activities that we were interrupted by the arrival of Phoenix. Actually his arrival had been most timely for the last few screws were giving us some trouble. After brief introductions all four of us set about finishing the task, this time with three people pushing on my back and shoulders on the word go. Slowly, a sixteenth of a turn at a time, we got the last screws out and removed the board. The building was now open and we entered.

We just stood there for a few minutes taking it all in, the space, the windows with light streaming in from all sides - the sight of a mothballed public library, the scene of a crime. Then without further ado we leapt in to action.

I made no conscious decision to get involved and start working with Phoenix; once again it was intuitive and unquestionable. I took an instant shine to this colourful fellow. I could see immediately he was intelligent and erudite, but more than this he had a deeply ingrained set of moral values, he knew what was right and wrong and he stood up for what he believed in. A man after my own heart. Although he was charismatic and undoubtedly had the 'gift of the gab', he was no procrastinator or ditherer – he was a man of action, and when required, a man of direct action. He was also good with people, you could say a bit of a charmer. In fact I came to think of him as a bit of a magician. Certainly I could never imagine myself being able to energise and motivate local people, the 'Barnetenders' as he referred to them, to the point where they would link hands, form a circle around a tree and visualise good energy for the library.

The master plan was to occupy this building as a squat and re-open it to the public as a library, something of a first in Occupy history. This would hopefully highlight the newly introduced, unjust and draconian laws on squatting rights and the totally unnecessary cuts to public services that we were all being persuaded were absolutely unavoidable by the morally corrupt establishment.

Early days perhaps but we set about the tasks in hand. The first thing that Phoenix did was to get the electricity bill transferred. It was a definite no-no to 'steal' electricity. I wasn't paying that much attention but he then got busy on the phone, doing what he's good at – networking – trying to get fellow occupiers to spread the word and brief the media and so on. I got on with what I'm good at – practical matters. I set about checking the building over in order to render it safe and fit for public use. I took the boarding off the rear fire escape, checked electrics and water and started cleaning book shelves. One strange thing I found was that when the building was abandoned the central heating was left on at full blast, not the best way to treat either the building or the boiler and a complete waste of public money.

Things were now happening thick and fast but at this point, Thursday afternoon, it was still unnervingly quiet. A trickle of people had appeared at the side gate including members of the local press but people seemed loath to enter the now open public building. Labour councillors appeared at the gate to show support but were under instructions not to enter the building. It quickly became apparent to us that if this project were to succeed we needed to have the support and involvement of the local community and this wasn't happening fast enough for my liking at this stage.

As it happened, a Save Friern Barnet Library Group meeting was scheduled to take place that very evening in the British Legion building on the other side of the green. As the library was now open it seemed logical to hold this meeting inside the library so we started to put this idea into the ether. As far as I recall, Joanna Fryer was keen on this idea and was trying to persuade her colleagues to enter the library. Although there was some resistance, for a while it seemed as if this would happen. However, by 7:25 pm when no one had appeared at the library we deduced this wasn't going to happen, so Rosie, Phoenix and myself set off across the green to the British Legion building.

We were welcomed into the meeting and of course the main item on the agenda was the occupation, or the "squatters", as they were referred to. It quickly became apparent that there was indeed resistance to the idea of entering the building, Maureen Ivens, the then Chair, was saying that they couldn't possibly get involved in anything "illegal" and that they couldn't endorse either the occupation or any SFBLG members entering the library. I was quick to point out that entering the building wasn't illegal. It wasn't against the law and it wasn't a crime. It was purely a civil matter and as such would require someone to take civil action in a court of law, which, even if it went ahead, was unlikely to have any repercussions on anyone from SFBLG. I was backed up in this by Phoenix and a knowledgeable chap (whose name I forgot) who was a law student. In this case common sense and bravery did not prevail and it was deemed too risky and illegal for SFBLG involvement at this stage. I was silently flabbergasted but worse was to come. When it came to the second half of the meeting we were actually *asked to leave* as we weren't members of the Save Friern Barnet Library Group!

I remember to this day my sense of bewilderment, disappointment, anger and hurt as we walked back across the green. Incredible, the guys that came to save the library being asked to leave the Save Friern Barnet Library Group because they weren't members. Phoenix, of course, being Phoenix has learnt to take this sort of thing in his stride and marched forward undeterred. He is much more stoical and resolute and I think I took some comfort in this. Rosie's way is also not to do a lot of verbalising, so this minor, and as it would turn out, temporary setback just seemed to float away in the cool evening air.

When we got back to the library, Daniel and Petra had arrived and food was being prepared. I got to know Daniel, who would become the 'caretaker', quite well in the coming weeks. He is quiet but strong, and reliable like an oak. He has great perception, not just about politics, economics and situations but also about people. Daniel knows who is a good egg. He has a wonderfully dry sense of humour. A man of few words but great power, in some ways diametrically opposed to Phoenix but also a very likable chap. The vibe inside the library was quite different to where we had just been. It was quiet, peaceful and quite dark, as candles had been lit. It was a place to chill, to reflect, to eat, to get to know friends better and for some, a place to prepare to live.

I cleared the rubbish from the back yard, generally tidied up and went to get spare keys cut. But by the end of the second day the place was still quiet, people were reluctant to cross the threshold. We planned a community open day for Saturday. I organised the first event to be held in the 'new' library, a slide show and movie presentation – 'Thunderbirds Are Go' for the kiddies and 'The Waterways of Finchley' for everyone else. The turnout for my shows was not that good but they happened and people were starting to come in to the library bringing all sorts of donations, not just for the library but also for the occupiers who were now beginning to be seen as conquering heroes.

The coming week was very busy. Books were now pouring in, being donated by locals. I found some metal bookshelves in bits in a shed out the back and started to put them together. I went to the Barnet Furniture Centre just round the corner in Queens Parade to see what was available. The manageress, Bernadette, kindly donated some tables and chairs and we installed these. I also went to Compton School because the grapevine had said that they were getting rid of loads of chairs, which they were. Phoenix was busy with the media, the Butterfly Circus as I call it, and I left him to it. Things were happening fast and people were now entering the library.

In the midst of all this there was something on my mind, and it was on Phoenix's as well – the front doors were not yet open. We had to sort this out, so when things became quiet at the time when afternoon turns to evening, we turned our minds to it. No problem. We picked up some tools, went out front and dealt with the two additional locks that did not have keys. 15 minutes later we opened the front double doors. Daylight flooded in. In one fell swoop the building was somehow more alive and also more legitimate. In the space of just ten days, this project had turned from a damp squib to a soaring success - the building was now well and truly occupied and open.

THE MAGICIAN

PETE PHOENIX

I'm an environmental and community activist. I've been squatting for twenty-five years and have helped to set up and organise numerous eco community projects. One of my favourite activities is getting into empty buildings and sticking stuff up with blue tack. Making a community centre out of whatever you can find around - transforming buildings and spaces – this is my passion and what I love to do.

Over the years I have squatted in flats, shops, warehouses, churches, mills, community centres, hospitals, mansions, schools and now finally a library. I was first drawn into the fantastic tale of the Friern Barnet literary resistance as I walked down the bustling streets of Camden. I was rung by Pedro of Occupy News Network who I had worked with at Occupy London's Bank of Ideas and the occupied courthouse in Hoxton. He told me that a few people some of whom I knew, including Dave Skipper, had occupied a library in Friern Barnet. There was a large local campaign and they really wanted to save the library.

I decided to head up to Friern Barnet the next day, 5th September. This was a few days after they had brought in the new law on September 1st about criminalising squatting in residential buildings, which I believe to be extremely undemocratic. The Government ignored their own public consultation in which 96% of the replies did not favour criminalising squatting, including submissions from the Police Federation, judges, lawyers and homeless charities who all said do not criminalise. They added a small clause on to the end of the legal aid and sentencing of prisoners act saying it was a crime to trespass in an empty building with intention to live there. Thus they removed an ancient right to shelter that we all have or had in this land. Squatting in non-residential buildings is still legal i.e. shops, warehouses, pubs and libraries providing they have *never* been lived in.

An MP called Mike Weatherley and Finchley and Golders Green MP, Mike Freer, began an early day motion to outlaw and criminalise squatting. The cause was taken up with a highly orchestrated campaign of lies and propaganda pushed by the Evening Standard (The Evil Standard), the Daily Mail and Torygraph. The government then pushed for this policy to be implemented. In the meantime, the squatting community had organised Squattastic meetings, networking events for squatters about the new law. The re-creation of the squash campaign, (Squatters Action for Secure Homes) www.squashcampaign.org was a resurrection of the squash campaign of the mid-nineties when the government last tried to criminalise squatting.

In the last stages we followed the parliamentary process very closely. We saw the hollow shell of a sham democracy that is now run and steered by corporate lobbyists. Corporations are rapidly taking over our democratic system. As a prime example, Mike Weatherley has been paid £160,000 by the Landlord's Association and estate agent/property developer companies. He has declared this in the parliamentary book, but is this customary? Is there any link between property developers and a law that will force people onto the streets or into the over-inflated rental market to fill up rooms and spaces for estate agents? No one knows the exact figure of how many people squat, it's estimated to be between 20-50,000 people in the UK. Squatting is one of the oldest forms of land tenure, occupying a place and working there.

Dave and his friends were squatting in a residential property nearby and were looking for a non-residential place where they could squat because of the change in the law. This new legislation means that the police can kick the door in and arrest all the people in a residential building that may have squatted there for many years. So Dave and his friends thought they needed to move. Dave used to come into the Bank of Ideas and bring loads of bags of skipped food. So the posse called him Dave Skipper. It was only when he squatted in the library that he revealed he was an ex-librarian, so he became Dave the ex-librarian Skipper. Community projects help to bring out peoples' many hidden talents, and we've a web that strengthens community. So when I got to the library, a squatter John stuck his head out of the window and said hello. I said how do I get in and he said we haven't got a doorway yet. I then met Dave and a guy called Mr Greenacres who I assumed was the third squatter as he steamed forward in a direct action style removing the boards on the back door.

Mr Greenacres, it turned out, had been a long-term library campaigner and an expert on green spaces in the borough as well as a cycle campaigner. Luckily, the council had left us a set of keys in the keyhole of the back door and Mr Greenacres excitedly started to explain some of the complex story of 'Barnetenders' and the library campaign. I grasped the short story that this had been a library and a village green since the

1930s and that the local people had vehemently resisted the council from shutting it down due to the unnecessary cuts of the austerity robbery programme.

Mr Greenacres said we should link up with the Save Friern Barnet Library Group. Then I found out from Dave that unbelievably, the council had been in and offered them space in another building - in Friary Park House. It was unheard of for councils to be offering something so quickly. Something very strange was going on. The Council obviously wanted to get the squatters out very, very quickly, before the local campaigners linked up and issues arose for the council.

I got Dave and his friends to write down everything the council had said because this could be useful in a future court case. The council had given them a lift in a car up to Friary Park and showed them round the building. They said they could have one big room as a community library, which was about a quarter of the size of Friern Barnet.

Mr Greenacres, Rosie (another campaigner), and I then went to the Thursday night SFBL meeting where it was explained that nobody wanted to use Friary Park House because it was in the middle of a park with no lighting, difficult for old people, no disabled access and anyway, people loved the Friern Barnet Library building. The SFBL meeting was in the British Legion where we met Keith, Maureen, Frances, Alfred, Ollie, and Kim - beautiful people who've helped to save this library and campaigned for a long time. Alfred's story in particular, is an incredible one. He's coming from Rwanda where he lost some of his family and his home. His children really need the library for their education and it's close to his flat. I appreciated his story that as a single parent with five kids, it was more difficult for them to get on a bus and go to another library.

We found out a bit of the early story and did our best to listen and get the picture of the campaign for the library that had now been ongoing for some time. Some of the SFBL group were very enthusiastic. They wanted to come in on the Saturday as we said we'd be opening it up on that day for a trial. But some had reservations about the legality of entering the building while it was squatted. We tried to allay concerns explaining that squatting in non-residential buildings was still legal and that our group would hold the building over the next weeks hoping to facilitate some kind of negotiated solution for saving the library.

I got in touch with Daniel and Petra, who had originally come from Hungary and now needed somewhere to live. They were willing to occupy and sleep in the library for most of the time; in fact they were anchors of the early rota occupation. 'Big up' the Hungarian team. Others started to arrive; Pedro and some of the other Occupy people, Leon, Mark and Donnie, who we had worked with at St Pauls Occupy,

27

the Bank of Ideas and the squatted courthouse in Hoxton called Occupy Justice.

We started to do what we always do when we first enter a building and that was to tidy up and organise. However there wasn't much tidying up to do because what we found was one very large room of empty wooden bookshelves, a lobby, small kitchen and a toilet and the echoes of many memories of hours whiled away, entwined in other worlds that books take you to. We organised regular Monday morning meetings – a standard practice in most of our projects over the last fifteen plus years. The intention being to get organised early in the week and keep the campaign and various activities on track.

Initially there had been phone calls from council officers offering amongst other things the use of Friary House, so I rang the council informing them we had prepared a letter, which we then emailed. In it we told them we were interested in their offer of another building; that we were caretaking the library building and we were happy to meet and discuss matters with them. We added the standard end that we add to all of our negotiation letters and have done for years: 'Looking forward to a mutually beneficial arrangement.' The council were keen to meet with us, which was a really good sign for negotiations. They wanted to meet on the following Monday. I tried to put it off until later in the week but they were insistent, 'We want to meet you on Monday'.

I did a clever thing. The Council thought they were going to meet with four or five squatters. Having been to the SFBL meeting, and discovered there was a massive amount of local interest we needed to build an alliance with all these groups. So I invited SFBL, the local bloggers and anybody else concerned to the Monday morning meeting as well as Diane, a freelance Guardian journalist. Four council officials turned up; Julie Taylor, Mike Fahy, another woman whose name I didn't catch, and another guy from Commercial. They were faced with a roomful of twenty people, sitting in a circle, some of whom were obviously bursting to express their strong opinions on the library. We got them to use the Occupy method - direct democracy hand signals - basically one finger up to talk (just like at school); two fingers for a direct point; wavy jazz hands for agreement and consensus; a fist in the air for a block of a proposal - but you'd better have some good alternative ideas. So I helped to facilitate and discuss some sort of solution to saving the library.

The council officers agreed to meet with us again the following Monday which amazed me, because in effect it gave us a licence to occupy the building for one week. The meeting went ahead the following Monday and one of the best lines was from Mrs Angry who mildly ranted at the council, 'Why has it taken the squatters to come into this building in order for you to get together and actually listen to the people you are supposed to represent?' The council were definitely on the back foot.

Right at the end of the meeting, somebody had a massive outburst. He went off ranting and shouting, 'But we haven't sorted anything, they're not going to give us the building, there's no arrangement here, we haven't sorted anything out.' When I asked who was shouting, I was told, 'that's Mr Reasonable'. So I met Mr Reasonable - one of the famous five bloggers - and Mrs Angry, who was there putting her very interesting spin on things.

We had a further meeting the following Monday, another at council offices and yet another at South Friern Library a couple of weeks later. We tried to get the council to be reasonable, to speak to the people they are supposed to represent, and to let us use one of the 1.4 million buildings that stand empty around the UK.

The media circus heated up, there was a lot of press coverage, and radio and TV broadcast including the BBC. In fact, this occupation had gone global. We were getting TV coverage as far afield as Australia, China, Sweden and Japan. At this point we had a lots of locals coming in to help and support the burgeoning 'community library'. We had filled the place with books, furniture, equipment and computers, and mums and kids, and lots of people were now using the place.

THE REVOLUTION'S HERE!

ROSIE CANNING

When I first heard that there were squatters in the library, I was confused. Squatters in the library? Surely not. It was probably just security guards sent by Barnet Council. Until I saw what was happening with my own eyes, I didn't know what to think. Thursday, after work, I decided to make the effort and go straight to the library. I knew there was to be a Save Friern Barnet Library group (SFBLG) meeting in the British Legion. When I got to the library, it still looked deserted, so I went round the back. I knocked on the gate and shouted over and was most surprised when Mr Greenacres appeared.

It was a strange feeling walking into the library through the now opened back door. I found myself behind the issue desk, in a space usually reserved for library staff. The first thing that struck me was the emptiness: the empty shelves that looked so sad and the dark brown wood that seemed to clash with the blue-grey carpet tiles. It was strangely hollow and spooky. But something was happening. There was a certain vibe in the air. Mr Greenacres was chatting to a couple of well-spoken young men who used words like protest and occupy. One, with blond dreadlocks, was smiling and saying they were there to reopen the library. His name was Phoenix and he told us he had a long history of turning disused buildings into community centres. I looked at the empty shelves and laughed. But the earth was shifting on its axis and soon the impact would be felt all over the London Borough of Barnet.

As mentioned, that first evening there was a meeting of the SFBLG and confusion as to whether the meeting was going to be held in the library or not. When nobody turned up at the library, we decided to go to the British Legion building across the green where they usually held their meetings. Unfortunately, the meeting didn't go that well.

Not everybody was ready to embrace Phoenix and his friends unlike Mr Greenacres, who had immediately grasped what this could mean.

'We have to support them,' he said.

'But they're breaking the law,' someone else said.

'I've spoken to the lawyers, and we have to keep our distance', said another.

'Trespass is not a criminal offence,' said Mr Greenacres.

I was keeping quiet, most unlike me, but I didn't know what I felt at that moment. It all seemed rather surreal. We left the Save Friern Barnet Library meeting a little frustrated and downhearted.

The following Saturday, SFBLG held their weekly pop-up library under gazebos on the green. Some of us had decided to go one step further for by now we had realised that this was an opportunity too good to miss. I announced Greenacre Writers would be holding a Creative Writing Workshop inside the library. Mr Greenacres planned a screening of his slide show, 'The Waterways of Finchley,' and the Occupiers invited everyone into the building for tea and biscuits.

That first Saturday, ironically, there were more people outside the library than in. More Occupiers had arrived though. One of them, Daniel, told me this was how it was.

'People will come', he said. 'It is always like this to begin with.'

He annoyed me, just a little, with his laid-back positive attitude. Barnet is not a positive place to live. It feels as if we have been living in a war zone for many years. Except we don't use bullets - words are our ammunition.

Here in Barnet, we're lucky to have the *Famous Five Bloggers* who were praised by Eric Pickles for their work in holding Barnet Council to account. Sounding very unlike Enid Blyton characters and more like characters from *Cluedo,* Mr Reasonable, Mrs Angry, Roger Tichborne, Citizen Barnet, and Mr Mustard spend their time keeping a very close eye on what Barnet Council gets up to.

Back in the library, I asked Daniel what he did for a living.

'Oh, start revolution. We started in Hungary, and now they are okay. So we come here.'

A revolution!

I was to be part of a revolution? In some ways it felt as if I had been waiting for this to happen all of my life - ever since I was at secondary school in the seventies when there was a huge amount of social unrest. One day, we decided to walk out of our classrooms and go on strike. It was a time when we only had electricity three days a week and had to live by candlelight at night. They were exciting times.

There is something deeply intoxicating about people being alive, awake, and taking control of their lives.

Rumours were circulating, *trespassing is illegal; the squatters broke in and damaged the property.* They hadn't. They climbed in through an open window and found all the keys inside. And then Mr Greenacres opened the front doors to let the light and people in. This one act changed the ambience of the closed library. Articles began to appear in the local press and suddenly the national newspapers were involved, *The Guardian*, then the BBC and ITV. Barnet had hit the big time. We were all famous. Even I had my few seconds of fame when I appeared in the *Big Issue*. My head was spinning.

Meanwhile the lukewarm reception from the community was, as Daniel had predicted, hotting up. Slowly at first, but as the local groups and people began to stream through the now-open front doors, the shelves were beginning to fill up. Even more surprising was that Barnet Council officers had immediately entered into negotiations with the Occupiers. This is a council that usually plays a game of consulting but does not really want to know what the people of Barnet want. They often think up ways to be as illusive and difficult as possible. We were all gobsmacked when two days after the Occupiers arrived, council officials offered Phoenix and friends Friary House as an alternative venue for a community library.

Councillor Richard Cornelius, Leader of the Council (at the time), told newspapers:

> *"We have been trying to encourage community libraries in the borough for some time. If this group would genuinely like to open one in Friary House half a mile [SIC -1.5miles] away, we would happily give them the book stock."*
>
> *[Times Series: 5/9/12]*

I'm sure I'm not the only one who felt torn by this statement, for several reasons. I work in a medical library as a Senior Library Assistant. I've used libraries all my life. I do not believe in volunteers running public libraries. In fact, when I think of the highly paid executives in this borough, the amount wasted on consultants who seem to breed in the corridors of the North London Business Park and then expect library staff to become volunteers and work for nothing! I see colours: red, purple and blue; and the expletives that escape from my mouth would make a hardened criminal blush. There can now be no doubt that this government wants to end public services, the National Health Service, and everything in between. Not just that, it wants to recreate a new order, one of slavery but without the feeding or housing of its slaves; a sort of feudal system but without the rewards. Oh, hang on, a slight exaggeration; these volunteers will get an award, a certificate, or a badge of honour. Sixty people in Enfield, volunteers in the library service, recently received these nonsensical decorations. I imagine our borough officials will shortly be doing the same thing here.

Just a few months before the occupation, I had been visiting Mill Hill Library and saw some leaflets, '*Become a library volunteer – Your Library Needs You*', mimicking the old war-time poster, 'Your Country Needs You'. The leaflet went on: '*Are you enthusiastic, energetic and love your local library? Would you like to gain new skills, meet new people and contribute to your local community?*'

I knew immediately what this meant and spoke to a couple of the library staff. I asked if they were worried about their jobs. One of them was quite open and said yes, but in that sort of accepting way that many Barnet employees seem to have. Another immediately said, 'Sorry, I'm not allowed to comment'. I replied, 'Well when you don't have a job anymore, you may wish that you had'. Little did I know that all library staff had been warned not to talk about the closures, otherwise ironically, they had been told they would lose their jobs! I took handfuls of the leaflets and *said* I would hand them out, all the while knowing that it was a futile demonstration, as they would just print even more.

Soon after the arrival of the Occupy Movement, we heard the incredible news that Barnet Council would be reducing library staff by an unbelievable 24.5 posts, leaving just six librarians. They would be removed from libraries and relocated to Barnet Headquarters, the Business Park. Librarians in a business park and not in libraries! What Alice in Wonderland nonsense was this? By the end of October 2012, these staff received letters of their jobs being 'at risk'. None of these posts were held by the corporate or execs. This also meant that the employees with the largest salaries were not at risk. These were the front-line professional librarians who were losing their jobs - the intention being, to create a library service with a small number of qualified staff plus a large brigade of volunteers. These cuts are not necessary; they are just an excuse to axe public services, close public buildings, and eventually privatise the National Health Service.

It must have been about a week after the occupation, as the shelves in the library were filling up with books and the Occupiers were becoming heroes, that I wondered if it might all turn sour. Would the community turn against them in a sort of *Playboy of the Western World* scenario but with multiple playboys being driven out

33

by the community? This fear subsided after the very unpopular announcement of further job losses in our libraries.

Negotiations with Barnet Council went well and a meeting was set up on the 10th September, inside the Library. The meeting was attended by three very senior council officers, members of the Occupy Movement and members from the local community. It was the first of its kind in the Borough of Barnet being arranged by the community and not the council. We all sat in a circle, some on chairs, some on baby chairs and some on the floor. Unbelievable, but what fun we had!

Highlights of the meeting included: Solutions and dialogue from Phoenix. A reminder that Councillor Robert Rams was on his honeymoon. And apparently Richard Cornelius, the leader of the council, would be happy to be involved in Rams' absence.

Mr Greenacres was quick to point out there could be no compromise over relocation – it would be like taking the heart out of the community. This library was purpose-built, therefore it would be difficult to replace.

Mrs Angry asked why it had taken the occupation of the library for the council to start negotiations and added, 'Doesn't it set a precedent for squatters?'

Mr Greenacres brought up some valid and important points about council accounts: In 2012/13, the council said it saved £110,000 by closing Friern Barnet Library. Not true, said Mr Greenacres, due to the costs of running 'artsdepot', the interim library service. £34,200 in rent alone, as well as the closing down costs of the library, removal of books, refurbishment of the new space plus a librarian at artsdepot – therefore the council could not have saved £110,000 that year.

Somebody wondered about the Carnegie Trust. Surely the library was built for the people for as long as they wanted it, in perpetuity. And even more crucial, was this on the deeds? (The deeds, it seemed were conveniently missing.)

I asked if, as the recent consultation showed, 73% of residents didn't want a library at artsdepot, then why close North Finchley? Keep it open and reopen Friern Barnet as an interim solution. Surely, much money could be saved by this measure.

'Solutions and dialogue', said Phoenix.

And so it went on. Roger Tichborne reminded council officials that some older people use libraries to save on their heating bills; in fact they use libraries to stay alive.

Not having a 'complete handle' on who uses the library, Julie Taylor (Deputy Chief Executive of the Borough), reminded everyone that the library had been closed to improve literacy.

I thought Mr Greenacres might explode at that moment, but he was quite calm when he said, 'You closed this library to improve literacy! Excuse me while I fall on the floor.'

Mrs Angry asked; was the council intending implementing eviction procedures?

Julie Taylor quickly reassured everyone that the council were 'not making any snap decisions on that.' Which proved to be a blatant lie as we subsequently learnt that the proceedings had in fact started the day after the occupiers arrived.

The meeting eventually came to a close. Phoenix thanked everyone for attending and ended with a reminder about 'co-operative negotiation, solutions and dialogue'.

I had offered to take minutes at this unusual meeting, and I quickly typed them up and circulated them. They were to become a historic document, the accuracy and layout were commented on and the 'snap decisions' would later be referred to in court as a symbol of the council's 'license' to the squatters. I didn't understand any of this furore at the time, as to me they were just minutes.

THE CARETAKER

DANIEL GARDONYI T.

I had just arrived in England after hitchhiking back from Hungary with my girlfriend, Petra. I had been away for six months organising the Occupy movement in Hungary. Things had escalated. Hungary was turning into a dictatorship so we were creating a resistance. On my return, I contacted Phoenix to see if he knew of any projects, but he didn't. In Kentish Town we went into a charity shop, Petra had never seen anything like this before. There are no charity shops in Hungary but there are shops selling English second-hand bullshit clothes. I was just standing there when Petra pointed and said, 'Isn't that the guy from the videos'. I turned around and saw Phoenix.

He was making a phone call and was walking up and down for about ten minutes. 'Hello there, we're winning', etc., etc. When he finished his call, he asked me, 'Do you want to live in a library?' I said, 'Fuck yeh'. So the next day, we said goodbye to our squatter friends in the Castle Squat in Kentish Town and headed for Friern Barnet. We took the 43 bus from Archway to Friern Barnet where the library was waiting for us. We entered by the back door and found Phoenix, Mr Greenacres, Rosie, and John already there. It was dark but there were candles. It felt nice inside the library, we had noodles and tea. We had to spend the night there. I was really tired, but we had fun talking and Petra was playing chess and beating everyone.

We put the call out for our friends to come and help us run the library. We just wanted to open it up and turn the building into an alternative community centre, which is what we usually do. For the first few days, local people wouldn't come in but then something magical happened. It was on the Saturday, and suddenly people arrived. They started coming in, they were curious, and Phoenix helped them feel more comfortable. I was chatting to them and then we all went outside and joined hands around the tree. We projected good energies into the tree to help us and wish us a good library project. Mr Greenacres had organised a slide show on green spaces and some of the community came inside the library because they were curious. Other people were still scared to come in because they thought it was a criminal offence.

Early the next week, Mr Greenacres and Phoenix opened the front doors and daylight entered. More and more people came in with books, food, computers, chairs, and tables. The Furniture Centre in Friern Barnet turned up with some tables and chairs and Fiona, one of the local community, turned up with a fridge.

I had started squatting after two years of slaving in London. I was always a rebel and a kind of a freedom fighter, but I didn't care about the economy, just injustice that made me feel horrible in general. Budapest was too stressful and the brainwashing of mainstream politics turned people against each other. To go even further back, I was starting to be a full time comedian when my genre ceased to exist. I had learned acting, drama history, dramaturgy, film studies and I was just beginning to get recognized. Then shit happened and my traditional Hungarian theatre-based cabaret ceased to exist. It was the same people in power as now; they somehow killed comedy for seven years. No theatre wanted to do it anymore. We call it Absurdistan. Comedy was dead until they imported the American stand-up variety in bars which is a consumerist version with full control and censorship on TV.

Then I came to England. I worked in restaurants at weekends, and during the week I was doing a McDonalds slave run. I spent all my savings on a shitty room and moved in with an old 'friend' and other depressed Hungarians. I can still see them now, sitting in a circle, heads hung low, moaning. I almost had no time to sleep, and even like this I was falling behind with the rent, almost starving to death. I only ate some porridge every other day. Some days, even if I had money, I was too tired to cook and eat. I had to move from the apathetic Hungarians. I had two choices: get some petrol from the car wash that was on the side of the house and make it hot - or start squatting.

So I started squatting with some new friends, who had been 'couchsurfers'. Couchsurfing is not squatting. You find a host, they welcome you without charge and they show you around. It's against the stupid type of tourism; you see the reality of places; you get to travel and it's for free.

I didn't know anything about squatting, but I knew it couldn't be any worse than my previous existence. So I found some friends and we started squatting together. We learned the hard way on the go and my former neighbour from Wembley joined us too after a few months. He became the Jamaican granddaddy of squatters. Our crew grew from three to five, then we joined other friends and our numbers were around fifteen. Then we merged with another squatter tribe and occupied an old nursery with thirty people.

Suddenly the callout for 'Occupy Everywhere' happened in 1000 cities around the world. I was invited to occupy the London Stock Exchange on the 15th October, 2011. I was a bit late, having got stuck in South London helping a friend, but when I got there and saw the Saint Pauls camp, it swept me off my feet. The things I had kind of given up on and thought I was alone with were being reborn in front of my eyes. I even started washing dishes at the kitchen tent, just to contribute in any way I could! So, I had started on the path that would eventually lead me to Friern Barnet library.

About a week or so after moving into the library, Petra and I heard some thumping noises on the roof in the middle of the night. We were half asleep and couldn't work out what it was. We thought maybe it was cats fighting on the roof and we went back to sleep. We were in the middle of a period of good dry weather and didn't think anything more of it at the time.

After about another week, roughly two weeks into the occupation, it started to rain. I remember that it was Petra, Donnie, his girlfriend, Stefan and me. We had been watching a crazy Canadian-German series called Lexx. We heard louder and louder splashing noises as the rain outside got heavier and then we saw that the rain was literally pouring into the kitchen and the staff room. I called Mr Greenacres immediately, but I don't think he believed how bad it was until he came down the next day.

Mr Greenacres said the roof seemed like it was damaged on purpose. It was damaged so the rain could just pour in. Most of the lead was still there along with boot traces so he thought of sabotage. He showed us the photos taken on the roof and it was really badly damaged, so I thought it was plausible. Usually until I have solid evidence I try not to jump into conclusions. Still I can easily imagine the roof being vandalised to cut the occupation short or to make the building useless so the council could sell it easily.

Living in the library was like St Francis of Assissi. We were all like St Francis, our communities were similar in so many ways. I've visited a Zen Buddhist monastery back home in Hungary and it was also very similar. We only had a few hours to ourselves at night and there was only one room we could sleep in, plus one to use for discussions while others slept. The kitchen had a sink, an electric cooker and a microwave, so we were able to cook food. There was central heating in the building so we didn't have to feel cold and the local residents were kind enough to offer us their showers and washing machines. In an ordinary empty building, we would have built ourselves a shower but there wasn't a suitable space in the library. The library was not like any other occupied building, we had a service to run but we had experience in running occupied community centres, so we knew we would manage somehow.

In the first seven to ten days there was round the clock security surveillance, three shifts a day, sometimes two guards at night sitting in a car. We worked out this was costing about £5,000 a week. The security guards were pulled off after a while. Looking back it seems ironic that there were security guards outside guarding a supposedly closed and empty public building for more money than it would have cost to keep the library open. And all the while we were inside carrying out our caretaker duties to the best of our abilities.

My first impressions were that the people of Friern Barnet were lovely and they must love that building. I saw they were shy at first with us, but then they started trusting us. We were the caretakers so we felt like the caretakers. I often look back on this story as I talk about it in different countries. In Hungary, I'm still doing my best to help organise the resistance to oppose the same evil that is destroying communities and all forms of life. I'm just one of the many droplets of water that creates the flood.

HEROES OR VILLAINS?

DONNIE VORTEX

We are not superheroes. The Friern Barnet Library was, of all the projects I became involved in, the one where we did the most good and had the best luck. But, we are not elite trained activists. We attended no secret camps for 'guerrilla librarians'. We are more or less ordinary people who, under the extraordinary circumstances of these times, leapt at the opportunity to save something loved. We were catalysts; the people who made it happen were the volunteers, the book donors and all the people of the Friern Barnet community, who had the courage to take back what is rightfully theirs.

This is the saga of the Friern Barnet Library through my eyes. The eyes of a squatter, an activist, a guerrilla librarian and, despite what the tabloids would have you believe, a normal person - not a drug addict, a 'parasite', or a 'scrounger'. I was born in South-West London and my mother grew up very close to Friern Barnet. I went to school and then university to study politics but left when I realised that it was a poor substitute for engaging in the issues of the day on a practical basis. I remember days of paralysis, watching the Jasmine Revolution unfold on social media, whilst no-one in the faculty wanted to even discuss it. I remember leaving and the waves of relief washing over me when I saw it was possible to actually *do something*.

Last August I was bouncing around North London, often staying at a squatted garden centre in Camden but mostly living in a dilapidated mansion on Primrose Hill, dubbed the Haunted House. Around that time, as part of our online media project Occupy News Network, we covered the Julian Assange case, live-streaming through the night when police nearly stormed the Ecuadorian embassy, long before the mainstream media got there. In his speech, Assange spoke of those who 'brought the eyes of the world', that was us.

After the media circus had died down I sometimes slept at the garden centre. More than a place to stay, I needed a project to sink my teeth into. I'd returned to London from Hungary with a renewed appetite for constructive activity. I rang Danny to ask if he and his girlfriend Petra had found a place to stay and was pleased to hear that they'd moved into a building that needed extra crew. At this point I didn't know exactly what I was getting into.

When I arrived, it was dark outside and light blazed boldly through the windows onto the street. At that time the main room of the library was just a wide expanse with no books and just four chairs. Phoenix was there and pleased to see a new arrival.

I spent time with both Petra and Danny whilst in Hungary, the country of their birth, and had lived with Danny in the past. Petra had never left Hungary before. When they met there, she had decided to travel with him, like a Doctor Who companion. She was a New Age style of woman with instant love and hugs, tarot cards and smiles. I couldn't understand much of what she said though and over the course of our stay attempted to teach her some English.

I spent a lot of time in the library but on one of the nights I wasn't there, Danny and Petra told me they'd heard someone up on the roof making a lot of noise. We didn't think much of it at the time but a couple of weeks later when rain started pouring in the building, we realised the significance of the noises. We speculated on the possibilities of lead thieves or of the council trying to literally sabotage us.

Donated books started pouring into the library at initially an encouraging, then a slightly alarming rate, to the point where much of our time was taken up shelving and sorting the books with the aid of the local volunteers. Several were trained librarians and clued us up on the various problems facing the profession. In addition to the library closures imposed, without public backing by the coalition there were a dwindling number of jobs in libraries with many of the positions now being filled by volunteers. People get degrees in Librarianship for a reason. That's because most positions require a great deal of knowledge of the whole spectrum of the written word to know instantly whether a particular work resides in Romance or the Literature section and know by heart the books that are 'must-haves' for any well stocked library. So we decided to make it clear from the start that the aim of the project was not just to keep the library open but to have funding fully reinstated and of course, the hiring of a trained librarian.

I was warmed by the near instant show of support and acceptance we got from members of the public. People wandered in from the street, wide eyed and amazed, saying, 'I can't believe it's open again.' They told us how they used to bring their kids there after school. When we told them we were squatting in the building, they didn't seem to mind in the slightest.

Normally, no matter how civil and well intentioned we are to our neighbours, or no matter how pro-social the project, we struggle to gain acceptance and support. People are afraid initially, imagining a crack den or a criminal hideout has opened up in the street. After a few reassurances they still remain suspicious, but after a while they may begin to treat us with an attitude of curiosity and neighbourly acceptance. Usually locals fall a little short of actually supporting us, but in Friern Barnet support was whole-hearted and near instantaneous.

It wasn't long before we were visited by BBC Radio and the *Evening Standard*. They arrived early in the morning and Danny went out to speak to them while I roused myself. He came back in saying, "The *Evening Standard* guy, he just told me he doesn't know what to do. Because it's like, 'Oh squatters, bad, we don't like them.' 'Ah, but libraries are good. So he doesn't know what to do. The BBC guy wants someone to do an interview."

Danny is Hungarian and usually speaks quite well, but he said that it would be better if someone English did the interview. I am usually a little uncomfortable talking to the mainstream media, however, I reluctantly agreed to the task. I was to do the interview by radio linkup with Vanessa Feltz in the studio. I messed up almost immediately due to some feedback in my ear from the sound equipment. Predictably, she asked me whether the running of libraries was something that could be done by volunteers or whether 'any old person from Kingston-Upon-Thames could do it', which seemed to me a rather snide remark. "Yes, I think anyone can do it." I said "Provided they have the proper training, support and funding. We have the support here from several trained librarians, who are helping us to put the books in order and to run the library in the proper manner. Still there are limits; we are doing the best we can within them."

I had dodged a few bullets. She then asked whether we were just looking for a place to live and if we would leave the library if it was handed back to the community. I replied that I was there to see the project completed and then to move on to the next one. I was relieved when the interview ended without having fallen into any of the verbal traps nor getting angry at her sardonic tone. Still, I felt like I had only just scraped through. So when supporters started arriving and telling us what a good interview they'd heard on the radio that morning, I was pleasantly surprised.

We organised 'People's Assemblies' and invited the council officers who had originally closed the library to come and negotiate with us. The meetings were attended by many angry Friern Barnet residents and bloggers as well as the local media. Phoenix usually took on a facilitating role, which, more often than not involved holding back the angry locals to stop them from ripping the council officers to pieces. However, it was necessary to keep the council in a dialogue without ruling out the possibility of giving up the library, whilst also talking about what we really wanted: the return of the library to the community.

Many people brought a lot of excellent research to the meetings, including Mr Greenacres who brought a proposal for how the library could be run a great deal cheaper than it had been. The questions of executive salaries were also broached. If just one of the senior officers took a pay cut, the library could be saved. For the most part the council officials sat uncomfortably on tiny child-sized chairs. For once they had to listen to the people they purported to serve. When they spoke, they hid behind a wall of lies and bureaucratic doublespeak, which they were caught out on numerous occasions. Despite being public servants, they refused to be filmed, saying that it would 'change the nature of the conversation'. As ridiculous and spineless as I have ever seen human beings stoop.

On the other hand, the Labour councillors who supported us were having a fine time, attending the meetings but rarely getting involved. With much enjoyment, they watched the officers squirm. We, the Occupiers, and other friends from the movement didn't speak too much either. As we saw it, our role was not to divert the locals from their chosen course of action but simply to hold the space and provide information when necessary. Phoenix, however, had a strong idea of how things should go, having presided over numerous assemblies and squat cases. At times, it verged on the autocratic, but the plan was working well.

Sometimes, one wondered if it would just be better to let the locals have their say and deliver the verbal beating that the opposition deserved. But that would have resulted in a room of screaming Barneteers and a possible beheading. So, it was better to divert the course of the meetings towards constructive engagement, negotiation and to constantly hold out the hand of reconciliation - a hand which the council consistently failed to clasp.

From time to time we got stories back from Barry Rawlings and Pauline Coakley-Webb, the two Labour councillors, about how council meetings often descended into hair tearing and screaming on the subject of the library. We'd only been in the library a couple of weeks when we heard that Brian Coleman, ex-mayor and Tory councillor for Totteridge, had assaulted Helen Michael, proprietor of Café Buzz, on North Finchley High Road. We found it epitomised the standards of behaviour amongst that insidious lot and indicative of their own deep hypocrisy: Helen was filming him contravening parking rules that he himself had put in place. I regarded our adversaries as half clowns and half bullies, who had somehow risen to positions of power and were continuously digging pits for themselves.

Mark 'The Weaver' arrived at the Library, a familiar face from Occupy London. He's very good at handling the media and we pulled off a real coup the day the BBC requested a visit. On the phone they said they were very keen on filming our sleeping space. We agreed but on the day of their arrival, we packed away our sleeping bags and mattresses and tidied the library as we did every morning. Then, we calmly waited for the residents and various supporters to arrive. When the BBC crew got there, with their presenters, technicians and all their equipment; they found a tidy, well stocked library, with volunteers, readers and children running around, with us behind the desk stamping out the books. They had clearly expected to see bearded hippies strolling around in their pyjamas, empty beer cans and dog ends lying around, that sort of thing. Instead, they found something completely different and were forced to run a very different story, one of 'lovely middle class people' versus the bureaucratic, out-of-touch council.

I'd like to thank all those who brought donations of food to the library. At first, we salvaged food that was past its sell-by-date from the skips behind the Co-op, but soon this was no longer necessary. Supporters brought a near constant supply of fresh, delicious food, sometimes harvested from their back gardens and allotments. Meal times were an absolute delight, with sometimes up to ten people crammed around the table in the library main room. Laughter and hilarity were always on the menu. Often, we'd get visits from members of the campaign group and invite them to feast with us. As the weather grew colder, I began to spend long hours making the perfect winter soup.

Some of this may give a sense of what a cosy, friendly atmosphere developed in the Library. By now the heating was on and we had a chess board, tables and big comfortable chairs. The shelves were now completely filled and we had to get new shelves in. I often spent quiet moments reading whatever caught my eye. I was particularly excited whenever a rare old beauty was donated. I would go to the place where I'd gathered them altogether, open up the case and pour over gold embossed leather, and ancient ink illustrations, smell the crisp yellow pages and read the notes penned by ancient gift givers, some more than a hundred years since. A library is a shrine to the written word, a place of reverence and knowledge. Living and working there gave me peace and clarity from the moment I awoke and emerged from between the shelves until when I slept between them once more.

There were events most days of the week; reading groups, open mic nights, and even a book signing. The author, Will Self had been mentioned in several meetings. It was suggested to invite him because his latest book, *Umbrella*, was set in the old insane asylum almost opposite the library. So I got in touch with his agent and sent off a few emails. However, I was more or less brushed off and in the end it turned out that Rosa De Souza, one of the local library supporters, had a friend who was acquainted with the man. She then got in touch with him and to our amazement, he agreed to come for a book signing in November.

I felt confident to leave on this high note and was not surprised when a few months later I received the message that the library had been returned into the hands of the community. We now have a way to fight against the cuts and the wholesale hijacking of British democracy by reinstating the community as the basic political unit.

We are squatters, activists, ccupiers and we have a contribution to make. We are often mocked, demonised or ignored, but we are people with solutions. We are not motivated by greed, fear or ambition but the desire to improve things. As people, we are really no different from most. You too could be the catalyst. Anything that we can do, you can do equally well. Climb through an open window, occupy a building, fight a campaign to save it, and win.

THE HISTORY OF FRIERN BARNET LIBRARY

DORRELL DRESSIKIE

Friern Barnet Library, housed in a Tudor style building in Friern Barnet Road, was opened in 1934 by the Middlesex County Council Library Service. A purpose-built library, it was among the first to be built and fitted out under the County Scheme for whole-time lending libraries. Before the opening of the library, books were bought and stored in school rooms and in church hall cupboards and the lending was done by volunteers, mainly teachers. They managed the service from the cramped confines of their school rooms, with opening times varying from one to two hours once or twice a week.

The Public Libraries Act 1919 signalled significant changes for library services. Middlesex County Council, as the Authority under the Act with responsibility for library services in its education area, inaugurated the County Library Service and with the Education Authority, set up a sub-committee to consult on the provision of libraries. The outcome of the consultation was the scheme to provide libraries in districts too small to maintain their own library service, and where those districts, in further consultation, showed interest in such a scheme.

At this time the population of Friern Barnet was 15,818 and interest in the County Council Scheme led to a meeting with Middlesex County Council Library Service to discuss the formation of a local branch. Friern Barnet Library Committee was formed and talks began on how to adopt the scheme in the district. This new committee acted promptly with a request to Friern Barnet Urban District Council to allow space at the Council Offices, The Priory, for use as a library. A room was allocated, furniture and equipment put in place and contact made with the Middlesex County Librarian for the supply of books.

An honorary librarian was co-opted from the County Library. A library of 1,200 volumes opened on 10 December 1923 in The Priory,

46

situated at the corner of Friern Barnet Lane and Friern Barnet Road. Opening sessions to the public were 7pm to 9pm, every Monday evening. The service proved to be in great demand. The number of borrowers increased rapidly as did the number of books borrowed. This led the Library Committee to request permission from the Urban District Council to allow more opening sessions. Tuesday evening sessions were introduced and were soon followed by Wednesday and Friday afternoons, 2.30 to 4pm. The librarian was assisted by volunteers from the local community.

At the third Annual General Meeting of the Library Committee in December 1926, the librarian reported an increase in membership, with 368 new members in the year under review. 1,374 books were in circulation and the largest number of books exchanged in one session was 675. The representative of the County Library Service present at the meeting commented favourably on the work of the library and added special compliments to the efforts of the librarian and the local volunteers.

The Library Committee considered other facilities that could be offered through the service. One favoured suggestion was for public lectures, but with space at the Council Offices already cramped, such activities would have to be held elsewhere. So began the process of finding suitable venues, lecturers and topics. Holly Park School was the first venue and the topic of the first lecture was *The History of Friern Barnet*.

Despite the support of Friern Barnet Urban District Council in accommodating the lending library at The Priory and the excellent work of the librarian and volunteers, there were a number of concerns. The space allocated for library use was far from adequate due to substantial growth in membership and the increase in the stock of books. The librarian and her volunteers were dealing with long queues of borrowers in cramped conditions. In addition, continued occupancy of the room at the Council Offices was by no means assured. A sub-committee was formed to draft a scheme for the acquisition of a new library centre. They were charged with finding a suitable site, estimating the cost and preparing plans.

Minutes of the Local Library Committee meeting on 18 July 1929 reported the findings of the sub-committee. The Urban District Council had proposals for road widening on part of an area along Friern Barnet Road. Completion of the project would leave land between Ramsden Road and Macdonald Road that would be adequate for the proposed new library.

Approval by the County Library Service to acquire the proposed site was reported in minutes of the Local Library Committee on 28 May

1931. The area measured approximately 5,700 square feet, and the price advised by the District Valuator was £600 with an additional cost of £50 to cover stamp duty, registration fee and legal expenses. The County Architect, W T Curtis FRIBA, took charge of design and contractors Messrs Allen Fairhead & Sons Ltd were appointed to undertake the building work.

The laying of the foundation stone on Saturday 23 September 1933 was quite an occasion. Guests assembled on the site between Ramsden Road and Macdonald Road for a service of dedication by the Rector of Friern Barnet, Reverend E Gage Hall. The choir of St John the Evangelist led the singing of the hymn *All People Who on Earth Do Dwell* and the foundation stone was laid by the chair of the Local Library Committee, Councillor C H Barber. The prayer of dedication by the Rector followed. The occasion concluded with guests moving on to a marquee on the lawn in the grounds of The Priory where tea was served.

In the following year, on Friday 23 March 1934, the Friern Barnet Branch Library opened to the public. The opening ceremony, held in the presence of a large and distinguished gathering, was chaired by County Alderman H S Button, JP and Chairman of Middlesex County Council. The library was declared open by Lord Elgin, Earl of Elgin and Kincardine, Chairman of the United Kingdom Carnegie Trust, an organisation promoting the development of rural libraries. The full descriptive note of the Friern Barnet Branch of the Middlesex County Libraries prepared for the opening ceremony was read by Mr C H Barber:

"The library building is planned to accommodate a lending section, a reference section, a reading room and a librarian's room. The lending section is designed on the "open access" system and this portion, in common with the remainder of the building, is capable of complete supervision from the librarian's desk, which is centrally placed.

The building is designed in the Tudor style, the exterior being faced with multi-red facing bricks with stone quoins, mullions, transoms, etc. The roof is covered with handmade sand faced tiles. The windows are metal casements with leaded glazing. Oak wood blocks have been used for the floor, the shelving and fittings also being of oak. Electric heating on the "Thermovent" principle has been installed and lighting is also by electricity.

An electric clock, gift of Miss Mary Chambers, forms an important feature in the centre of the gable of the front elevation, and another electric clock, the gift of County Councillor and Mrs C H Barber, occupies a central position in the interior.

The building has been erected to the design and under the supervision of the County Architect, Mr W T Curtis, FRIBA and Messrs Allen Fairhead & Sons Ltd, of Enfield, whose tender amounted to £3,782.

The Trustees of the Carnegie United Kingdom Trust have generously made a grant of £1,140 to the Middlesex Education Committee for library purposes, and this has been utilised towards the cost of the Friern Barnet Library."

There was a special tribute to the Honorary Librarian, Miss Mary Chalmers, who, since 1926, had worked at The Priory venue. The team of volunteers were commended for their tireless work and active service that helped to make the day possible.

The first book issued from the new library was a copy of *Story of San Michele* by Axel Munthe. The borrower was Mr A C Henry, Chairman of the Friern Barnet Urban District Council and the book was issued to him by Lord Elgin. The stock of books on the opening was 8,060 classified under the headings of non-fiction, fiction and children. Opening hours were 10am to 9pm, so planned in order to allow extra time for people returning home after their day's work. Pupils attending local schools were allocated a special section within the library and for younger children there were afternoon sessions of two hours from 4.20pm to 6.30pm, except on Saturdays. The temporary libraries at The Priory, Holly Park School and St James School were closed.

In addition to lending books, the library service provided a range of other facilities for borrowers. New books were displayed and book exhibitions were organised. Musical evenings were held and seasonal holiday programmes put on display. Newspapers, trade journals and some periodicals were placed for the benefit of readers. Local organisations were allowed space on notice boards to advertise community activities, particularly if the activities were considered educational. Minutes of meetings of the County Council and the Urban District Council were also placed for public view.

In a desire to have facilities for young readers developing in parallel to those for adult readers, Middlesex County Council Education Committee proposed extension of the library to include a separate children's room. Before such proposals could be taken forward, however, it was September 1939 and the outbreak of war with Germany. The library had been operating from 10am to 9pm but early in 1940, in compliance with blackout regulations, closing time was changed to 7pm. By October 1940, Friern Barnet Library Committee reported that early closing would continue and, due to enemy action, could give no forecast on possible change. Other planned activities were also affected. The Local Library Committee cancelled its meeting of December 1940 but could set no date for future meetings, and this led to the shutdown of some other activities.

In wartime, however, the value of the library was well demonstrated with a record rise in the number of borrowers. Reading and listening to the radio became the only recreational activities that could be enjoyed, resulting in the increase in demand for light reading material from borrowers. Troops and all members of the Armed Forces located in the district were granted full privilege to use the library and batches of books were sent to Army Auxiliary and Searchlight Units stationed nearby.

After the war, the proposal for an extension to the library to include a separate children's room was not pursued, but the County Library Service did request permission from the Urban District Council to lay flower beds in the land adjoining the library. The council provided seats outside the library for public use. The public garden area, with flower beds and benches on the Ramsden Road side, was in place by 1948.

The gradual resumption of normal activities was evident in the librarian's quarterly reports which detailed the book stock, number of borrowers, the daily issue of books and increase in use of the library, especially by children from local schools. The Library Circle resumed its programme and musical evenings with gramophone recitals were held. Some local organisations such as the Workers' Education Association and local Ratepayers' Association used the library for some of their meetings. New opening hours of 9am to 8pm and early closing at 1pm on Wednesdays were introduced. A caretaker post was approved and arrangements set out for routine cleaning of the library.

In March 1955, the library celebrated twenty one years since its opening. The celebration was reported in *Muswell Hill Mercury and Highgate Post* on 1 April 1955, under the heading 'Library's 21st Birthday'. The distinguished gathering included representatives of Middlesex County Council, Friern Barnet Urban District Council, local organisations and some of the guests who had attended the opening ceremony in 1934. Chief among them was the Earl of Elgin, who had travelled from his home in Scotland for this occasion, saying on acceptance of the invitation, '*One always answers an encore.*' Councillor A. C. Barber, who had been Chairman of Friern Barnet Urban District Council in 1934 and who had borrowed the first book, announced to the guests that he still had the book in his possession. Middlesex County Council Library Service had done a special binding of the book and had presented it to him as a memento. The Librarian and staff at Friern Barnet were credited with their professionalism. There was special mention for the project they had pioneered to allow borrowers free access to book shelves to select their own books. That had proved quite significant nationally and gained so much popularity that it was copied internationally.

Career exhibitions were held for school leavers. Younger children from nearby schools were given instructions on how to use the library. Books were sent on loan to the nearby Friern and Halliwick hospitals. Reciprocal lending arrangements with other libraries in Barnet allowed borrowers access to the service elsewhere. Members of Friern Barnet Library could, for example, borrow books from the North Finchley branch in Ravensdale Avenue.

The County of Middlesex disappeared in 1965 due to boundary changes. Friern Barnet Urban District, along with the local authorities of Finchley, Hendon, Barnet and East Barnet, became the London Borough of Barnet. Barnet Council Library Service then came into being. Working closely with the Education Department and the Borough Librarian, it took on responsibility for all libraries in the Borough. Friern Barnet Library expanded its services to meet the changing needs and demands of its users. Special Children's and Teenage sections were added, class visits by children from Holly Park and St John's Schools were encouraged and for very young children there were Story Time sessions. There was choice of audio books, videos and large print books and a range of leaflets and pamphlets with information on various community activities. Some equipment, such as small chairs and toys for the children's area, were provided by the Friends of Barnet Borough Libraries.

1965 also saw the celebration of the anniversary of V E Day. On display in the library was wartime memorabilia such as gas masks, posters, newspapers and photographs. With choice of background music, the event was like a recall of the mood and sentiment of the war years. The book *Barnet at War* was on sale and its co-author, local historian Percy Reboul, was on hand to sign copies for visitors. A garden party was held on the adjoining lawn. Wartime food was the order of the day with Spam, corned beef and cheese sandwiches "issued only on the surrender of coupons from a simulated ration book", copies of which were on sale and were snapped up by visitors.

The Friends of Barnet Borough Libraries was founded in 1988 by Councillor Frank Gibson, one time Mayor of the London Borough of

Barnet, to create community awareness and support for Barnet Libraries. A non-political group of library users, the Friends worked through a central committee and over the years raised funds to supply extra amenities such as coffee machines and to assist with some library activities. Members of the Friends were present in 1994 to join staff of Friern Barnet Library in celebration of what was defined as the "pensionable age" of the library, its 60th year since opening. Children from Friern Barnet schools took part in the celebration with craft activities and Story Time. One visitor, aged 83, who had been using the library since the opening in 1934, had the honour of cutting a birthday cake. Perhaps, quite appropriately for that year, the library was redecorated and had an access ramp installed.

Extensive property development in close proximity to Friern Barnet Library has been going on since 1997. Princess Park Manor was opened in 2007, Princes Gate Estate in 1998 and in 2000 the former Friern Barnet Town Hall was converted into residential flats. These developments brought new neighbours, many of whom were to discover an excellent amenity on their doorstep. The excellence of the library was evident in an exhaustive inspection of all Barnet libraries by the Audit Commission in 2001, resulting in a three star rating, the highest award for excellence. The Audit Commission Report stated then: 'the services have good track record of delivery and responding to users' demands. Staff and users share a strong commitment to improve the services'.

The library offered more than a book lending service. Library stock included CDs, DVDs, large print books and items in some community languages. There was a range of pamphlets, magazines, and trade journals. Users had access to computers, Internet access and info-link helpline and trained and experienced staff helped everyone to make the best use of the facilities. Local councillors held surgeries at set times in the library; there were monthly coffee mornings with speakers, always on a topic of interest. The very young and their parents had Rhyme Time sessions and children from nearby St John's School, who themselves used the library, were the carol singers at Christmas time.

Since its opening in 1934 and up until April 2012, the library had never closed down or had to be relocated. It was a welcoming library with staff on hand to advise and assist and, as one reader, commented: "I enjoy coming here; the comfort and convenience of the reading area. I browse through books, read up on daily news, pick up information on some local events and I find the staff always welcoming and helpful."

SAVE FRIERN BARNET LIBRARY GROUP

MAUREEN IVENS

The campaign run by the Save Friern Barnet Library group was enormously successful and this was thanks to the hard work and commitment of some outstanding local members: Tamar Andrusier, Ben, Frances Briars, Fiona Cochrane, Sheri Darby, Joanna Fryer, Harry Gluck, Michael Lunn, Paul Merchant, Alfred Rurangirwa, Martin Russo, Sarah Howe, among others.

It originated one day late in February 2011 when, on seeing the news in Friern Barnet Library of the Council's plans to shut it down, I felt a deep sense of outrage and immediately asked a couple of Friern Barnet Library users if they would join me to try to save it. The positive reaction I had from Alfred Rurangirwa and Frances Briars, followed by that of Lynne Barber and subsequently a student, 'Ben', allowed us to form an embryonic group. We were assisted, with ideas, by a friend who wishes to remain nameless and then by the trade union Unison, who provided us with badges and placards. They helped us with the printing of the posters we circulated in the first couple of weeks of existence to local residents, many of whom posted them up in their windows. Alfred and I organized a petition on the Barnet Council website. We knew we were having an impact when the Labour Party set up a petition to save the library and distributed flyers around the ward calling on people to sign it.

A small poster on the wall at nearby New Southgate railway station garnered a few more adherents, including a trained librarian, Fiona Cochrane, and we held our first public meeting in the library itself. We decided to hold weekly meetings. After a few sessions in the library where we were made to feel somewhat unwanted by the librarians – we relocated the venue of our meetings to an upstairs room in the adjacent British Legion. Having to travel abroad fairly frequently, I felt unable to act as Chair of the group and was delighted when Fiona Cochrane agreed to take up this position, which she held for a year. I acted informally as co-Chair and also Treasurer and then assumed the role of Chair when Fiona stepped down.

Sometime in April 2011 Tamar Andrusier, who was our Schools Officer throughout 2011, joined our ranks, to be followed not long after by Martin Russo (who became our Media Officer). In early May 2011 we held our first awareness-raising event at the library. It was one of a number of very successful public events that year, including the very well attended 'Walk to the Library Week' (for local school children). I argued in the group that we should focus on winning the support of a broad range of local actors from the outset. I wrote a submission, on behalf of the group, to the Parliamentary Committee investigating the state of the United Kingdom's library service. We were able to draw up two different proposals to run the library at no cost or little cost (as the Council requested) and held four meetings with Council Library Executives to discuss them. The local media started to run almost weekly articles about the campaign, and very soon the national and international media were featuring our fight.

We forged international links with campaigners in Stockholm and Granada in Spain. My aim was to embarrass our government abroad about library closures to build on national pressure. The Council finally rejected our proposals to run the library essentially because they no longer wanted to have any paid staff working in FBL. Having done this, we knew it was only a matter of time before they shut down the library. The last day of life (as it was supposed to be) of the library was the 5th February 2012. There was a cliffhanger of a meeting at Hendon Town Hall the evening before where, despite protestations from all sides (including the Conservative Councillor Kate Salinger) the unanimous decision was taken to shut it.

Travelling back that evening from Hendon, three of us in the group decided that we had to take part in a sit-in inside FBL the next day and we calculated (correctly) that the Council would bring forward the time of closure to lunch time. The five hour sit-in was held by five SFBL group members and members of the Barnet Alliance for Public Services. The campaign having gone on at that point for a year with much publicity, local, national and international media gave wide coverage to the story.

The following day the community awoke to a library that was boarded up. There was absolutely no question that we would give up. We decided to take up the idea suggested by the blogger Roger Tichborne to run pop up libraries on the village green next to the library. These were weekly events, come rain or shine, and we ran them from March through to August 2012. The pain and frustration of having our library shut, all the books stripped out was huge but at the same time the pop up libraries, with the attendant publicity, offered a great opportunity to embarrass the Council. I was especially keen for international media to focus on our events to maximise such embarrassment and the chances of a stubborn central government giving way on its philistine policy of undermining public libraries.

The following month the object of our frustration, our empty public building, was entered by members of the Occupy Movement and local Green Spaces campaigner Mr Greenacres, who reopened the doors to the general public. En route to an interview for a film about events in Barnet I received a call to say what had happened. As soon as I returned to Friern Barnet, I went to the library to shake hands with the squatters. However, their arrival was awkward in some ways: firstly, they knew little about the campaign or fights around the country against library closures. I argued in SFBL that we absolutely had to cooperate with them (a few of our group were not at all keen to do so) or the campaign would be lost. Cooperate we did although it was not easy.

The legal case to evict them led to the highly positive outcome of the library being reopened on a long term basis but along the way the lawyers felt obliged to concede that the library belonged to the Council (we had been arguing in SFBL that the local residents owned the building from a moral point of view, because it had been paid for a long time ago from people's taxes). In fact I argued, even further, as did others, that Councils acting to shut public buildings that provide essential services are ultimately guilty of theft.

The Secretary of our group, Joanna Fryer, independently had submitted an application for the library to be recognised as a community asset, which led the Judge in the case to recommend the Council negotiate with the local community over the library.

I was exercised over Barnet Council's plans to shut Friern Barnet Library, but what interested me just as much, if not more, were the reasons – I felt - why Councils, in general, should not respond to an admittedly very strong recession by taking measures which undermined the rights of citizens (at, moreover, the time when they need them most).

Having been unemployed for six months at one time I knew the pain of unemployment and I felt greatly motivated to save our library for the jobless who desperately need such places of calm with all they have to offer in terms of reading and leisure materials and, naturally, internet access. Children and young people were a particular focus of our campaign too, but we all felt in SFBL that the library was for all people, young and old, with or without disabilities.

Looking at issues around public libraries I found research from the United States showing that their closure often meant the disappearance of the last remaining public building in many, particularly poorer communities. In fact in Friern Barnet, the library's closure would have meant the end of any public buildings (the other two public building having shut down in the last twenty-five years). This, SFBL felt, would have ripped out the heart of the community.

Looking at statistics and details regarding libraries around Europe and many parts of the world, I found that the only other country shutting down public libraries in any number was the United States (Denmark also closed some country facilities) but the number of their closures was dwarfed by the scale of closures in the United Kingdom.

The United Kingdom, under the present Conservative government, is out on a limb when it comes to shutting public libraries. It also occupies the very bottom of the league of countries in the western world in terms of social mobility, something public libraries are uniquely placed to assist with.

Much of the anger we felt over Barnet Council's plans to close Friern Barnet Library (and its actual shutting of it) stemmed from the fact that this was a council following a line that had been taken by central government which consisted in undermining the country's public library service – surely one of our greatest cultural achievements. In so doing it flouted the law that is supposed to protect this valuable network (the 1964 Public Museums and Libraries Act).

Another strand of argument in terms of saving this building and its service was the economic: speaking to local shopkeepers I was taken aback by the scale of decline in their sales once our library shut down. What madness, I thought: just when the country's economy is highly weakened, why would a council (or councils for that matter) start to unpick the fabric of the local economy?

UP ON THE ROOF

MR GREENACRES

About two weeks into the occupation I received a phone call from Daniel to say that water was pouring into the building, literally pouring in all along the back of the building. Mr Greenacres inspected the building at the beginning of the occupation and found it in relatively good order. The roof was sound and the box gutters and flashing seemed to be in good condition and watertight. The only oddity was that a large skylight had been boarded over from the outside with a piece of Sterling board which had not been waterproofed. I must confess that when I was speaking to Daniel on the phone I thought he must be exaggerating, possibly there was a section of flashing that wasn't watertight and some rain was entering the building but it couldn't possibly be as bad as he was saying. By now it was late, pitch black and raining. I couldn't do anything till daylight so I did my best to calm him and said I'd be over the next day.

As soon as I got to the inside rear of the library I could see there *was* a major problem, there was evidence of substantial water ingress and staining. At the back of the building there is a parapet wall with box gutters running the entire length of the building between the wall and the roof tiles. When I put my head over the parapet wall I simply couldn't believe my eyes – someone had been up there and smashed the roof to smithereens, broken tiles lay in the box gutters, zinc and lead that formed the gutters and flashing had been prised or ripped away from brickwork, everywhere was deliberate and wanton damage and destruction. It really was a heart stopping and almost heartbreaking moment. I stood there trying to calm myself, trying to be intelligent and logical – but that only made it worse for as I regained composure I came to realise that there was only one explanation for the sight before my eyes – a person or persons unknown had deliberately set out to vandalise the roof and theft was definitely not the motive as virtually no valuable recyclable material had actually been removed from the roof.

I clearly saw a large twisted piece of lead that, although fairly easy to carry away, had just been left there. On one corner I saw damage to the tiles that was consistent with a well-aimed kick from the heel of a boot. Smashed and broken tiles had cascaded into the gully putting debris all over the valuable lead which would be counter-productive to theft. Any self-respecting thief will set out to be as swift, efficient and as quiet as possible – get up there quick, grab what you can and get out quick – and this is not what happened here. And this was not the work of mindless vandals, deliberate damage was the order of the day here and whoever carried it out knew exactly what they were doing. It was a commando raid carried out to cause as much damage to the roof as possible, thereby causing rainwater to enter the building which would make life miserable for the occupiers and also threaten the integrity of the building.

I subsequently learned that about a week earlier Daniel and Petra had been woken up by banging on the roof one night. They were half asleep and wondered if there was anyone up there. They thought that maybe there were cats fighting on the roof. Anyway they went back to sleep and thought no more of it at the time. This recollection, although a bit vague in detail is not vague in timing and to my mind pinpoints the vandalism to a night about eight or nine days after the occupation began which in itself is very odd. For the first week of the occupation security guards were posted outside the library. They were there, in shifts, twenty four hours a day. The guards kept a low profile and were not unfriendly if approached. After about a week they were withdrawn. The damage occurred a matter of days after the guards had been pulled off. Considering that the library had been shut, empty and unattended for five months before occupation the timing of this 'vandalism' is very odd indeed.

As I have said I have no idea who the perpetrators of this wanton vandalism may have been but in my professional opinion it is not the work of thieves, it is more likely to be someone who has a vested interest in the redevelopment of the building. I immediately supervised the starting of repair works, the debris was cleared, salvageable tiles saved, and repairs were started. Unfortunately through ill health I was unable to supervise the work to completion but the work has now been completed by roofing contractors and the building is now water tight.

THE LIBRARY WILL LIVE TO SEE ANOTHER LEIGH DAY

ROSIE CANNING

Those first few weeks of occupation were a heady business. So much was happening so quickly. Every day from 11am until 1pm there were 'Coffee and Chat', mornings, Tuesdays at 5.30pm were 'New Author Readings', and at 6.30pm, 'Pilates'. On Wednesdays I ran, 'Make Friends With A Book', a scheme devised by The Reader Organisation to encourage people to share books, often the classics. The group would meet, read, talk about the text, talk about their lives and have tea, - a most important ritual, the sharing of tea and biscuits.

Children started to trickle in through the library doors once more, for the 'Teddy Bears' Picnic' and 'Song and Rhyme Time'. Music became an integral part of the library week, with Open Mic on Thursdays, where bands such as *Dijitalis*, *The Hamptons* and *Blues of Cain* could be heard quite 'literally' bringing the house down while in the background people were still reading books!

There were French lessons for both beginners and advanced and on a Saturday, Chemistry lessons with local campaigner Ollie Natelson. We have to hope he wasn't teaching them how to make explosives! And while all this was happening the books were slowly coming in, being dropped off in boxes, in bags, from cars and even van loads. The shelves were beginning to fill. Saturday afternoons became communal debating time, with members of Occupy and other organisations talking about various issues, such as the new Squatting Law that had recently been passed to stop people squatting in residential buildings. There were wonderful discussions about all sorts of issues; personal, private and things like the Community Bill of Rights, a Public Assembly on Strategy and the Future and even Fuel Poverty. Emails, phone calls, meetings, there were hundreds. 'Get Involved!' was the cry. 'We need your help to save the library. Bring more books. We need more books, especially for older children.' We were also collecting toys, DVDs and CDs. We wanted people to volunteer for two hour slots to check books in and out, accept donations, etc. and send out the invites to come and meet us: 'We have organised meetings each Monday at 6.00pm - 7.00pm and don't forget to sign the petition!*

I seemed to become a sort of secretary for the library. This included booking events, making sure they were listed on the board in the library, making sure anyone working with children had been CRB checked, which for some of the Occupiers was a bit of a pain but they understood. They not only cooperated about that (after some lengthy discussions) but they also made sure the library was kept tidy and removed their tobacco and smoking equipment from the issue desk. I found it difficult to monitor this side of things because they could have just told me to bugger off. I think it was a good discipline for the guys. Suddenly they were in the public eye and had to be aware that almost anyone could walk through that open door. I put up notices about recycling and keeping the place clean.

As well as secretary, I became PA to Phoenix. He would suddenly phone and ask me to produce hundreds of bits of paper about news stories, emails from the council, timelines, and other bits of important information.

My other role during this period was to become a go-between for various groups. Anyone that has worked in and with community will be aware of the array of different personalities and agendas. I sometimes felt I was working for the United Nations. The council officers would contact me and I would contact the community. It was the same with journalists. I would get a call or email that the BBC or ITV or even a Japanese journalist, wanted to see the library and interview people. I would then send out the call via email. I would sometimes be at work and not able to attend hence I am not in many of the photos. But I was there in spirit, working behind enemy lines. The ability to communicate with various factions of the community was to be crucial when the legal battle commenced.

After the first court case was adjourned, I posted a photograph I had taken of Phoenix and friends outside the court room on Facebook and added: *Whoopee whoo. Adjourned 14-21 days!!!! 2nd October LBB Barrister said 'If no defence filed. Defence be debarred from defending this case'!!! Friern Barnet Library needs pro-bono lawyer.*

The following day I received a message from Richard Reeve whose mother had worked as a librarian in Friern Barnet Library. He said she had been keeping a close eye on the campaign and added:

'If your campaign is still looking for a lawyer, Rosa Curling at Leigh Day and Co. did some pro-bono work for Save Chase Farm. I think they only do pro-bono work in special circumstances, so you will of course need to convince them of your cause.'

I felt very nervous about phoning such a prestigious firm of solicitors but knew if we had any chance at all of saving the library, it had to be done. Taking a deep breath I dialled the number.

Rosa Curling wasn't available so I left a message. I didn't expect to hear back from them that day, but it was only about 5 minutes later when the phone rang.

'Hi Rosie, it's Rosa Curling, I've been following the story about the library with interest.'

I smiled; this was sounding hopeful. We chatted for a while and she said she would speak to her colleagues and get back to me.

When I came off the phone, I was overjoyed but quickly told myself off – chickens and hatching and all that.

I was at work the following day when I received a call from Ugo Hayter, a really chilled and laid back para legal. She had even squatted herself in the past. Really? Blimey, even though I thought of myself as a bit of a rebel, I suddenly realised I hadn't really lived at all. A Paralegal to Richard Stein who also supported squatters – Phoenix would be pleased.

She told me that an emergency meeting with barristers had been arranged on Monday and I was to attend with Phoenix.

'Could I possibly bring a few others?'

'Yes of course, just let me know who.'

The following Monday, Phoenix, Mr Greenacres, Joanna Delos, Fiona Brickwood, and myself found ourselves in the centre of London outside the offices of Leigh Day.

After the closure in April 2012, I was determined that we would find a way to reopen the library. I began that evening by setting up a new petition, not one that was about closure or saving a public resource but one that demanded Friern Barnet Library be reopened. The plan had been to collect 7,000 signatures to force the council to re-discuss the closure and their plan to sell the building.

PEOPLE OF BARNET - 1
BARNET COUNCIL – 0

FROM ROGER TICHBORNE'S BLOG

On Tuesday 18th September, we made our way to Finchley Court for a hearing brought by Barnet Council to evict the occupiers of the Library. There were about 30 local people along to support.

The court officials were slightly nonplussed by the huge turnout and were not sure what to do. Eventually we were ushered into the courtroom. Not everybody could fit in and some people had to remain outside in the lobby. Barnet Council's case was simple: the occupiers are trespassers and they must be thrown out.

Pete Phoenix made the case for the occupiers. The council had in effect granted a license by entering into negotiations with the occupiers. Until these talks have concluded, it is inappropriate to evict the occupiers. There are also issues with title as the council claim to have lost the title deeds. Given that the land was given to "the people of Barnet for the purposes of a library", and the occupiers have reopened a library, it seems that the council is on rather shaky ground.

The judge was clearly unimpressed with the arguments put forward by the council. The occupiers asked for two things, firstly for the case to be struck out. They stated that if this could not be done, then they asked for a 21 day adjournment to prepare. Given that the council had only asked for a ten minute hearing, there was not time to hear the arguments to strike out the case, so the judge agreed to the request for a 21-day adjournment.

The lawyer representing the council bumbled that this was unacceptable as the occupiers had "no proper case". His protests were summarily dismissed by the judge, who gave the distinct impression that the council had clearly not presented any compelling arguments to support their case.

The judge then asked for an estimate of how long the case would take. The man from Barnet stated that it would be no more than 30 minutes. Mr Phoenix replied that many people wanted to speak and there would be much complicated discussion of land title and legal points. He suggested one or two days. As the council had stated that there was no case, the judge had agreed that the hearing would be 30 minutes, but if a proper defence was presented, then the case would be adjourned for a full hearing. Given that there clearly was a very robust case, it seemed highly unlikely that a 30-minute determination would occur and the case will progress to a full hearing.

So, we have wasted everyone's morning. The occupiers are saving the taxpayer money, as there is no longer a requirement for security in the library costing £600 a day. The people of Friern Barnet have a library. Everyone has won, yet the council are still hell bent on this Quixotic charge against common sense.

There was an interesting footnote to the proceedings. The occupiers and their supporters adjourned outside for pictures and interviews with Barnet Press and the Ham & High. As these were going on, the lawyer from Barnet approached the group in a rather surly manner. He demanded that we gave his bag back. We all looked at each other in amazement. It appears that he put it down somewhere and had lost all of the papers relating to the case. It was quite clear from the reaction that people were rather insulted by the insinuation that we'd pinched his bag. We suggested that it might be more sensible to go back into the building and look for it.

That is typical of Barnet Council. They can't even look after their legal documents in a courtroom!

PHOENIX RISING

FROM THERESA MUSGROVE'S BLOG

Wednesday 10th October was the day that Barnet Council went to court, expecting to be given an order enabling them to evict the community squatters occupying Friern Barnet Library.

It was the day that Barnet Council were not given an order enabling them to evict the community squatters occupying Friern Barnet Library, and so the occupation continued, at least until the week before Christmas, when the judge ruled there should be a full hearing of both sides of the case.

In a courtroom packed with forty or so residents, occupiers, library campaign supporters, Labour councillors, bloggers and press representatives, we witnessed the extraordinary sight of a judge clearly intent on ignoring the pre-emptory expectations of the local authority and instead opening up the process to a fair consideration of the case. I say extraordinary: of course it should not be so, but here in Broken Barnet, any due process which works in favour of the people and not those who seek to use the process against the people is a pretty rare event.

Rob Booth, a reporter from the Guardian, came to Broken Barnet to observe the civil war that has erupted in this borough, and to meet some of the bloggers who have reported the astonishing sequence of events that continues to evolve, as residents rebel against the policies and actions of their maverick, lunatic, privatisation obsessed Tory council.

Before the court sat, quietly amongst the crowd waiting to enter the room, deputy leader and Tory councillor Daniel Thomas fixed upon the Guardian reporter and stood for a long 74 while whispering frantically to him, a relentless flow of One Barnet propaganda.

Mrs Angry stood listening, smiling to herself: whisper, whisper ... One Barnet is not just about two contracts ... there was no real opposition from residents, just a couple of cut and paste emails...

Booth nodded politely, but after a while his eyes glazed over, as if he might be considering jumping out of the window, and running as far away from Broken Barnet as possible. Who could blame him?

Once in court, Councillor Thomas found himself sitting surrounded by amused residents and campaigners. He looked distinctly uncomfortable. Barnet Eye blogger Roger Tichborne tried to make him feel welcome and encouraged everyone to applaud his courage in turning up. We did. He appeared a little unnerved. 'Councillor Thomas,' asked Mrs Angry naughtily, 'is Robert Rams not coming along too?' He swallowed hard, as the court tittered. He had no idea. Of course Rams, the Cabinet member for libraries, would not be coming, partly because he would probably not get out of the courthouse in one piece, but also because whereas we see a library still located in the community of Friern Barnet, the council sees only a property, an asset to be disposed of: a development opportunity.

Dan Thomas is in charge of such disposals and was there to reclaim his property.

Unfortunately for him, the judge thought otherwise, and once it became clear that there would be no triumphant statement for the press and photo of Cllr Thomas on the steps of the court waving his eviction order, he slipped out of the room.

Up to then the case had been pursued against 'persons unknown'. The judge, who was commendably helpful throughout, and really went out of his way to extend his advice and a full explanation of the process to the court, rearranged matters so that Phoenix and five other named individuals were the parties responsible for representing the library campaigners and residents. This may incur some costs, it was explained, and if so I hope that we will all do our bit by pledging some financial support.

The judge decided that, in view of the nature of the dispute, and the assertion by Phoenix and friends that the council had implied permission to remain in the library building, serious issues needed to be addressed, and this could not be done in the short amount of time allotted to the day's procedure. He began to mark out a timeline of dates in preparation for a hearing, including the requirement for disclosure of all documents by both sides, to each other.

Phoenix's adviser, his 'Mackenzie's Friend', Reema Patel, clarified that this would oblige Barnet Council to reveal the now you see them, now you don't, deeds of the library.

Barnet's representatives at court were completely wrong footed by today's developments. They had clearly foreseen a straightforward procedure, with permission given for an immediate eviction from the library premises.

When the judge offered them a chance of mediation, the council's solicitor took instruction and then refused, saying negotiations had been concluded.

On Tuesday, Phoenix and Rosie, one of the library campaigners, were sent an email by senior officer Bill Murphy, stating:

Dear Phoenix and Rosie, I write further to our meeting on 3 October 2012. There were a number of options presented to the Council as to how you proposed to run a community library at the former library premises.

Having carefully considered the various options the only viable option would be option 4 i.e. for the community interest group to purchase the premises. The premises have been earmarked for sale and the Council now need to market the premises for sale. Naturally, the community interest group can put forward offers for the purchase of the property at the appropriate time and the Council will consider that proposal along with any offers received from other interested parties.

It was made abundantly clear to the Council at the meeting by those who attended that the possibility of opening a community library from Friary House was no longer of interest. In order to consider any offers for the purchase of the premises the Council requires vacant possession. Having now explored all options in respect of your proposal to open a community library at the current premises the discussions are now concluded. The Council now insists that you give peaceful possession of the premises so that the property can now be marketed for sale. Once the premises have been put up for sale you will have the opportunity to put forward an offer for the purchase of the property.

Bill Murphy Assistant Director, Customer Services

Mr Greenacres, another campaigner, was reported to have been informed by Councillor Robert Rams that once repossessed, the library would be boarded up, and only one and a half days would be given to clear the building of books.

There has never been any chance whatsoever that any community group would be able to buy the library. Its stated value of £400k or so is nonsense: one could hardly buy a small house in the area for that - the value of this site must be several times that to developers, and the council will expect a price reflecting the maximum valuation. But oh dear: look now ... a development which no one expected. A judge prepared to listen to both sides of a highly contentious dispute, in which, as he observed, 'there is a public issue'...

The library was closed in April: here we are, six months later, under occupation by the community, and the council struggling to use the process of eviction in order to gain possession and flog the site to the highest bidder, as they are doing with our much missed Church Farmhouse Museum.

Many of the supporters left the court and made their way to the library, where Phoenix and friends laid on tea and biscuits and everyone celebrated the extension of life that this eighty year old library had just obtained: a stay of execution.

It is impossible not to like Phoenix: he is an engaging, energising individual, and yet enigmatic in his way. Who is he? Where does he come from? How long will he stay?

Mrs Angry watched him today sitting in the children's corner, and thinking with amusement of one her favourite childhood books, that he rather reminded her of a sort of dreadlocked Mary Poppins, (sorry, Phoenix) sent to teach us not how to fly a kite, but to teach a community to stand up for itself, and yes, like Mary, he is a stickler for good manners, isn't he, Captain Cooper? Jazz hands, and put your hand up when you want to speak...

In Birmingham, David Cameron was giving his speech to the Tory conference. Here in the people's library, nobody cared. Barnet was once a flagship Tory borough. The former seat of Margaret Thatcher, an easy-council: now it is the stamping ground of the sad, mad and bad right of the Tory party: the home of Brian Coleman, our former GLA member, currently on bail on suspicion of common assault, whose parking policy has brought the high streets of Barnet to the brink of economic disaster. Coleman, of course, was ultimately defeated by the concerted efforts of residents and bloggers determined to resist his re-election.

Friern Barnet Library was identified as a suitable case for development: this too has been obstructed by the efforts once more of a determined and well organised community. That leaves us with one more battle, one for which the occupation of Friern Barnet Library should serve as a very important lesson. That is of course the opposition to the £1 billion gamble of the One Barnet sell off of almost all our council services.

The library campaign is not an aberration, an issue in isolation - it is part of a much bigger picture. It marks a point whereby the residents of a community turn on the elected representatives who have betrayed their best interests and who have refused to listen to the very people they are supposed to serve. The shabby Tory councillors of Broken Barnet may not understand or care about the reaction that will ensue if they allow the One Barnet programme to continue. They may well, as the Joint Venture fiasco demonstrated, have lost control of the decision making process of the council, and allowed the senior management team of officers to hijack the agenda. The sudden departure of the Chief Executive certainly suggests that something has gone badly awry.

The companies currently vying for the £1 billion One Barnet contracts should take note. What is happening in Friern Barnet is just a taste of what is to come. The residents, activists and bloggers in this borough are not going to sit meekly by and watch their borough's services deconstructed and degraded by mass privatisation.

We will fight you to the last moment of signing, and we will watch you every day for the rest of your contracted tenure in our borough. One Barnet may be, as Ken Loach says in the new film, 'Barnet: The Billion Pound Gamble', a licence for exploitation: it doesn't buy our submission.

Don't say you haven't been warned.

Update Thursday 10th October 2012:

A statement by Barnet Council about the court case was quoted in the local Times: "*We have sought to keep an open dialogue with squatters through this process and we are disappointed that this discussion has been used to prevent the council assuming immediate control of a public asset. It is now unlikely that other councils will be as reasonable in their relation with squatters in any public building. This will mean we cannot have any further discussions about a community library until the court case is finished.*"

If ever you needed an example of Barnet's complete inability to communicate honestly and openly with residents, here it is. This story is not about a review of library provision, or even a rationalisation of resources. There is no rational and independent consideration of the needs of library users in the borough: the sale of

Friern Barnet library is purely and simply an asset stripping exercise, decided upon not on the basis of local need for services, or even as part of a budget plan - it is a suitable site for development, and, so they imagined, could be shut and sold without any electoral or political impact, whilst the cosseted Tory voters of Hampstead Garden Suburb would have their own ridiculous play-library subsidised as long as they want, no matter the cost.

That the people of Friern Barnet have taken back possession of something that is not a council 'asset', but a community centre, and one which belongs to them by every moral right is something to celebrate, and we should hope that their victory, however temporary, will encourage others to do the same.

Update Friday 11th October 2012:

Here is an amusing press release from Barnet Labour, in which Cllr Pauline Coakley Webb socks it to the increasingly desperate Tory deputy leader Dan Thomas:

"Deputy Leader slammed for Friary House "better access" claim Labour Coppetts councillor":

Pauline Coakley Webb has accused Barnet's Deputy Leader of making misleading comments in Wednesday's local press coverage that Friary House, in Friary Park has "better access" than Friern Barnet Library.

In response to the court ruling that the eviction of Friern Barnet Library "licensees" must go to full trial in December, Cllr Daniel Thomas was quoted saying, "We have offered a perfectly good alternative with better access but this has been refused by a small group who claim to represent the whole community." Cllr Coakley Webb slammed Cllr Thomas for his comments saying:

"Short of being in a parallel universe I do wish Cllr Dan Thomas would check out the facts before speaking. Anyone going to the Friern Barnet Community Library, currently being so well run by the community, would know that the perfectly designed slip road, right outside the library front door, has FREE parking and designated disabled places. Even if you came in a wheelchair the distance from the car to the front door is a metre or two.

Then there is a gentle short slope with handrails and there you have it, you are in the library. In comparison, Friary House, which Cllr Thomas has offered as a replacement volunteer library, is in the middle of a park. There is no car park on site so you have to find a parking space on the surrounding roads. You then have to walk to get to the park entrance, and then walk to the middle of the park only to then find a much smaller community space than is currently enjoyed at the original purpose-built, Friern Barnet Library!!

The truth is, Friary House has poor access, and is not wanted by the local community as a library space. Meanwhile, 4,000 plus, and rising, library supporters, is not what I would call a 'small group'. If that is a small group, it makes Barnet's Cabinet a dot on the horizon eager to be totally out of touch with the wishes of the community."

LOCAL LISTING

MARYLA ENEFER AND HELENE ALDERMAN

Maryla:

I believe (as in the case of a building) that a loss of a valuable historic structure is a loss not just for that particular community or me; it's a loss for everyone:

> *No man is an island, entire of itself; every man is a piece of the continent, a part of the main. If a clod be washed away by the sea, Europe is the less, as well as if a promontory were, as well as if a manor of thy friend's or of thine own were: any man's death diminishes me, because I am involved in mankind, and therefore never send to know for whom the bells tolls; it tolls for thee.*
> *John Donne*

I have been using Friern Barnet Library since the mid-1980s. And then my children used it. I heard about the closure at one of the Friern Barnet and District Local History Society meetings in early 2011. I couldn't believe the news and went to the library where it was confirmed. I heard about the petition and naively thought I could get friends and neighbours to sign it and the council would not close the library.

In June 2011, I went with my neighbour, Audrey Fairclough, to see our local Councillor, Mr. Andreas Tambourides. He was initially rather dismissive, saying the library was not in his ward and that the closure and decisions about it were nothing to do with him. I asked, "In that case, whose decision will it be?" He said the decision would be made by the 60, or so, Councillors. I gently made the point that, indeed, he would be part of the decision-making process.

He then picked up the phone and said: ...."Roberto, I have these two ladies that are upset about the Library closing - what shall I tell them?" He continued his chat while we waited patiently, then turned to us and suggested contacting Councillor Robert Rams about the consultation process.

I explained we had a petition and that I had collected 130 signatures. At that point, his tone changed completely. He took a copy of the petition and studied the addresses (to check that all were in his ward i.e. his potential electorate), pointing to those that weren't. "Cutbacks," he said and gave us the names of the other decision-making Councillors.

I had never met councillors before. It was a big eye opener as to how democracy worked in this country.

National Listing

Two local residents: Sheri Darby and Dr. Ollie Natelson, were applying for Statutory Listing of the Library building by English Heritage in autumn 2011. I knew both of them: some years earlier I had helped Ollie in listing Friern Barnet Town Hall.

Save Friern Barnet Library Group asked for letters of support for the listing to English Heritage. Anne Levens, one of my neighbours dropped off her letter for my information: it was so fantastic, that it set off a sparkle in my head and I knew I too had to write to English Heritage. I wrote two consecutive letters in support of the National Listing.

Sadly, National Listing was turned down by English Heritage in January 2012. To appeal was the next step.

However, on the 19th March 2013, the Department for Culture, Media and Sport decided not to overturn the original decision by English Heritage to list the library building.

My Personal Perspective

I felt so strongly about protecting the Library building. Apart from all the architectural merits and historical merits I felt the building had some tangible and palpable characteristics – something integral – I'm talking about things you can't quantify.

I looked through the eyes of a foreigner and I saw these things differently. I come from Warsaw. Towards the end of the war, Germans evicted all the inhabitants of Warsaw and started systematically detonating and blowing up all of the city.

Straight after the war, it was painstakingly rebuilt from student survey drawings, any surviving documentation and Canaletto paintings.

Having lost so much of their heritage, in Poland, even a simple building of similar architectural and historic quality such as Friern Barnet Library would be highly treasured.

I was also involved with the preservation of historic buildings and towns. I am an architect. I feel passionate about historic buildings. I was awarded a scholarship to the United Kingdom to study the repair and protection of historic buildings.

In Poland there was so much saving and preserving of historic buildings, and suddenly in this country, beautiful buildings were being demolished. It broke my heart to see that a country, so rich in historic fabric, and so, so lucky to have escaped much of the world wars' damages, could even consider pulling down such a valuable and important library building.

Over the years I have seen too many structures pulled down in this country and later on, people crying over their loss. Let's not make our successors cry over the loss of this little architectural gem – the Friern Barnet Library.

And also, let's not forget William Morris's wise words: *"These old buildings do not belong to us only...they are not...our property, to do as we like with. We are only trustees for those that come after us."*

Local Listing - the roller-coaster ride continues

At the beginning of May 2012 – the library was already closed by then, and its future was uncertain – there were rumours of the sale of the building and the green spaces to a well-known supermarket company. We collected signatures for another petition to reopen the Library and I personally collected well over 400 signatures. I helped with the pop-up libraries on the Green next to the Library building.

I was reading through various council websites when I discovered some policies on local listing,. It occurred to me that Friern Barnet Library was a perfect building to be locally listed.

I discovered individual people could propose a local listing – no forms, fees etc. I tried to find out who takes the final decision and was told, before mentioning the library, that it was decided by delegated powers i.e. the decision was made by a team of qualified, professional planners. It would be based on its merits.

The council tended to survey and look for potential buildings for local listing within conservation areas and look for additional buildings (they hardly listed any buildings outside conservation areas). It seemed quite simple. Then I was asked which building I was concerned about. When I said Friern Barnet Library – there was silence. Then the officer said, it could be quite a political decision and wished me good luck.

Two weeks prior to this, a very important document had been published, 'Good Practice Guide for Local Heritage Listing', by English Heritage. This became my bible.

Another thing that gave hope was that in the report for National Listing, the English Heritage Officer, hinted in his closing paragraph that although it didn't have national importance, it did have local interest.

Local Listing - the decent thing to do

Having discovered it should be a relatively easy process, I felt it was the decent thing to do. I knew it wouldn't necessarily save the building because Local Listing will not prevent a building from being demolished. However, it puts some restrictions on what can be done with buildings. In addition, applying for Local Listing would bring the Library into the spotlight of publicity.

I knew it would be very difficult to do this on my own so I approached Helene Alderman to help me.

Helene:

At our AGM in September 2011, many RA members "widely condemned Barnet Council's plan to merge the existing Friern Barnet and North Finchley libraries into a co-located 'Landmark Library' to be based in the Arts Depot building".

People in the community were also alarmed at rumours circulating about what would happen to the building. My RA continued to take an active interest. Maryla mentioned the idea of Local Listing and asked for my help. Although the process seemed simple, there were bound to be difficulties ahead.

I was impressed by Maryla's dynamic approach ... here was someone who had collected 200 signatures for our petition. The SFBLG had been started by a group of three: Alfred, Kim and Maureen and had grown from strength to strength, diversifying into different areas according to people's strengths. Maryla provided a new initiative. She clearly had conviction about the Library's importance to locals. I, along with many others, had pounded the streets from door to door, but had got nowhere near 200 signatures. Few people seemed to be aware that the library was under threat. Although the Council had produced a Consultation Document, the way the questions were framed was misleading and did not adequately give people a chance to express their disagreement with the proposed closure. Furthermore, the librarians, who were usually so helpful, were reticent in saying anything. We heard, much later on, that their jobs were under threat if they mentioned anything more than the date of closure.

Maryla's approach was invigorating and having, myself, worked on the Village Green application and various other initiatives, it was clear to me that she had the ability and knowledge to carry Local Listing through. We discussed whether she would apply as a concerned 'local individual' or whether it should be a group approach. We agreed, however, that there was not enough time for on-going consultation with others, but that we would keep the SFBLG informed and that anyone who wanted could be involved. As it so happened, everyone else was short on time, but long on interest!

Maryla:

I thought as we hadn't got the National Listing of Friern Barnet Library then at least let us try for the local listing. Having decided to apply for the listing as a private resident, not as part of the SFBLG, if anything went wrong I was prepared to take the responsibility.

But we only had a month to do it because I was going to be away for two months during the summer. It was the beginning of June 2012. Initially, I thought it would be very simple, however it took up a lot of my personal time and severely ate into my professional and family life for a whole month.

We decided to use documents that had been used before. This involved a lot of liaison, getting peoples approval and permission of copyright.

The fact that we were applying for the local listing seemed to set a complete precedent in Barnet as this was normally done by council officers, not local residents.

Helene and I spent many evenings going through council papers, editing, constructing arguments. Helene's skills with formulating the case, editing and proofreading proved invaluable. She worked tirelessly with total dedication.

I also had countless emails and telephone calls with my colleague Clare Wright (Chartered Town Planner and a specialist in developing solutions for heritage based initiatives), and colleagues in Poland. They gave me some fantastic ideas and advice. The document grew bigger and bigger and when complete totalled 100 pages!

Finally, we forwarded hard copies of the Application to three local Councillors. On Monday the 18th June 2012, I submitted it to Lucy Shomali, Assistant Director of Strategic Planning and Regeneration Environment, Planning and Regeneration at Barnet Council. All were hand delivered as it was such a big document.

We informed SFBLG about the submission and asked for help to make this public and get media interest.

Local Listing - Responses from official bodies

We then started the process of asking for letters of support from various official bodies, explaining what we were doing and chasing them up.

We received letters of support from:
- The Twentieth Century Society (C 20), a national amenity society "concerned with the protection, appreciation and study of post-1914 architecture, townscape and design."
- The Society for the Protection of Ancient Buildings, another national amenity society (1 of the 5) concerned with pre-Georgian buildings. In this instance they made an exception and wrote in support of our (much younger) Library.
- Friern Barnet & Whetstone Residents' Association
- Andrew Dismore, London Assembly member for Barnet and Camden expressed his support
- Friern Village Residents' Association

We also wrote to Theresa Villiers. Her role was very strange. We sent her copies of the original submission and her response was: 'I have been assured by the leader of the Council that this new merged facility will offer longer opening hours and would be open seven days a week.'

In my letter of response I pointed out that my submission did not refer to the library facility as such but to the historic fabric of Friern Barnet Library itself. I had learnt from previous correspondence that she took environmental issues to heart. I asked her to 'wholeheartedly' give her support for my nomination of Friern Barnet Library as a Local Heritage Asset.
I never heard from her again.

The council acknowledged the submission a few weeks later on 6th July 2012.

When I returned at the beginning of September 2012, I found a complete turnaround had taken place in the library. The Library was occupied by liberators. You couldn't invent a story like that. It was like new wave of hope for the community, an injection of new energy.

As the story of the library became so very political, I didn't expect a response from the council. However on the 10th Oct [no coincidence that this was the date of the second Court Hearing at Finchley Central about the ongoing occupation of the Library] I received a courtesy telephone call from a council officer about my nomination, to let me know how the application was progressing. This was a surprise.

I asked who would be making the decision and was told:
Cabinet Member for Planning – Cllr. Joanna Tambourides and
Interim Director for Environment, Planning and Regeneration – Pam Wharfe. It would be their 'joint considered decision'.

The officer hinted that the current political climate around the library should not greatly influence the historic importance of the building. So, it seemed there was a change of tune and that now, it would be hard not to make the case for local listing.

I was advised that if it was locally listed, it wouldn't secure the future of the building – it felt as if he were speaking to the whole community through me.

I wanted confirmation that the recommendation would be based on professional judgement. This was confirmed and the decision would be made by the end of the month.

The officer then said something strange and mentioned Theresa Villiers. She would be updated and be aware that they had kept me briefed!

After the phone call I was still very concerned, because the decision would be taken by ONLY two people i.e. rather than a committee or through a public consultation. Because of the court case and tense political atmosphere, I was worried that the decision would be political despite the professional judgement by local planning officers. I had faith in the professional judgement of planning officers but not the politicians. I thought that the decision making process should be broadened in such matters and that it should involve public consultation.

On the 28th November 2012, I received another phone call and was unofficially told that the library WOULD be locally listed.

The report hadn't been published yet. The officer reiterated again that the listing did not protect against demolition and that they would struggle to find somebody who didn't like the building. It was a very good case for local listing, he said, they always thought it was a good idea.

On the 4th December, the officer phoned again to say that Friern Barnet Library was added to the council's local list of buildings of architectural and historic interest. And that not many people could disagree that it was a very important building.

And that is where we stand today! After a long struggle, the building is still there and operating in the community, for the community.

As it stands today, Friern Barnet Library building has got status of a Local Heritage Asset i.e. it is locally listed.

But, perhaps one day, there will be a new application to English Heritage with 'sufficient evidence' that our library has "shaped this country's social, economic and cultural history".

History is still in the making...

THE LOCALISM ACT

INTERVIEW WITH JOANNA FRYER

How did you first become involved in the library?

I had been abroad for a couple of months and came back to discover Barnet Council were destroying my neighbourhood. They wanted to close the library, put up a telephone mast outside the old Town Hall and poison us all with the Pinkham Way Disposal unit. I went to a library party on the green and signed a petition. I also went to a meeting in June 2011. It seemed there was a lot of talk but not much action. The Save Friern Barnet Library Group was well intentioned and quite refined but I probably wouldn't have been so reasonable. I learnt how to be. Anyway, they needed a secretary, everybody sat on their hands, so I said I'd be the secretary. I was involved in every single meeting and every single event including the meetings at Hendon Town Hall that related to the library.

One of the reasons the library was saved was the successful application for listing the library as a Community Asset.

Yes, we had first heard about listing the library from our ward councillor, Barry Rawlings, who announced it as a small ray of hope at the Save Friern Barnet Library Group's AGM in March 2012. He said that in September 2012, the Localism Act would become law. This new act would require local authorities to keep a register of community assets and would give local communities first option to make a bid on any asset offered for sale. We were very cheered by this news. Little did we know then, that only a few days later Cllr Robert Rams would close our library over the Easter Holidays and pass the building over to LBB Property Services who would in turn pass it, and the surrounding land, to a property developer.

Given those circumstances what prompted you to make the application to Barnet Council?

As you know, the library which had been closed for six months, was reopened by the Occupy Movement in September 2012, and Barnet Council officers were engaged in weekly negotiations with occupiers and members of the community. A friend, by chance sent me a link to Locality, which helps members of the public to negotiate with their councils concerning the taking over of public services. Although none of us believed that we should be running public services since we were all paying Council Tax for just that, it seemed a chance worth taking and a back-up plan if all else failed.

How helpful were Locality?

Immensely! The young man, I spoke to, spent an afternoon researching links for me to follow. By evening, I had pages and pages of information on how to go about getting the building registered. He advised me to check Barnet Council's website in the first place to find their particular application process.

And?

Nothing. There was absolutely nothing on it regarding the Localism Act which by then had been law for a month. I tried ringing the council property and planning departments. One helpful person said, 'I don't know what you're on about,' and hung up. You just have to laugh at how crude it all was. I eventually managed to reach someone who was dimly aware of the law and said crisply, 'Yes, you will find it on our website in two weeks. Try again then,' and promptly hung up. I kept trying both online and by phone. Eventually, I reached a very kind voice in the Council who told me that it was now online and helped me fill in the application form. (There ARE some very kind people in those offices, despite appearances to the contrary.)

Was it a complicated form?

No, not at all. It was so simple that I sincerely doubted its effectiveness. It asked for the name of the group making the application, the constitution and membership of the group (any group has to have a minimum of 24 members), and reasons why the building should be listed as a community asset. I sent off the application on the 2nd November 2012

Was there any urgency?

Yes, we knew that the court case was coming up and it would strengthen our claim on the library if it had been registered as a Community Asset. It also meant that if the court case went badly for us, we could make a bid to buy the building. However, I don't believe that people who already own the building should have to buy it. All publicly owned property in the borough is legally owned by the Mayor and Burgesses of the borough. We people are the Burgesses. I telephoned the same kind council voice and informed her that the application was complete. She said it would take six weeks to process.

Six weeks?!
Yes, and even then only a stiff letter from our solicitors, Leigh Day to Barnet Council threatening judicial review and reminding them of their lack of action regarding our application form goaded them into action. It seemed to have an instant magical effect, though, and suddenly our lovely library *officially* became a Community Asset.

What date did this happen and how did you find out?
I received an email on the 12th December, 2012 telling me that the library had been accepted as a community asset. I was elated. I forwarded the email to everybody in the campaign. It was the first time that Barnet were admitting that the library itself was more important than a piece of real estate.

Editors Note:
The Localism Act requires local authorities to maintain a 'Register of Assets of Community Value'. This can include buildings or land that is considered of benefit to the local community and can be owned by anyone. If any registered asset comes up for sale 'The Community Right To Bid (Assets of Community Value)' comes into play. This basically aims to ensure buildings and amenities can be kept in public use and remain as an integral part of community life. The Act then gives community groups a six month period in which to develop a bid and raise the money to try and buy the asset when it comes on the open market. The important thing here is that there is a six month moratorium during which time a developer cannot move in with bulldozers. This will help local communities keep much-loved sites in public use and part of local life.

NOTES FROM A
MCKENZIE FRIEND

FROM REEMA PATEL'S BLOG

December 17-18th 2012

I'm passionate about literacy. About books, about writing, and above all, about the potential words have to change the direction of a person's life. That's why fighting for a library isn't just about fighting for a library. It's about fighting for opportunity.

I hadn't thought I would be sitting on the front bench at a County Court quite this early on in my fledgling legal career (as a McKenzie litigant friend of the defendant – to assist and to advise but not to represent). But doing so made an odd sort of sense.

It's rare for possession proceedings to make it through one hearing – let alone three, which was the situation at present. All judges have been mindful of one single factor – the need to give due weight to the public interest. They are to be commended for this fair and balanced approach.

These aren't mere possession proceedings. They are about issues that reach far wider than that. That's why we had German television, French radio and two staff from *The Guardian* present at the proceedings. And this dispute is much more about the judgments about our priorities we are making; at a local level, but flowing from national decisions – which are having national repercussions. Cameron talks about a broken society, but he is in part an advocate for that broken society.

We live in a world where the projected income of £400,000 for a large, beautiful and historic building is somehow worth more than the social value of a library. We live in a world where our public bodies and public officials appointed to those bodies flagrantly ignore standards in public life. And we live in a world where our public officials do not seem to understand that they are stewards of public assets; not owners of them, free to dispose of them as they will.

When the Occupy movement re-opened the library – they climbed in through an open window and did precisely that; run it as a library – not for the benefit of themselves, but for the benefit of the entire community. The level of support the movement attracted from the community, who donated over 8,000 books, are running Pilates and belly-dancing classes, music nights, and book signings, from the building is proof of the fact that – possession proceedings or no possession proceedings – the library is a focal point for the community.

The building itself also has a long history – and is inextricably linked to the community. It was given by the Carnegie Trust to the residents of Barnet some 100 plus years ago. The proposal that such an old, historical, unique building should be sold by Barnet Council despite fervent local community opposition and despite the fact the building was itself bought and sold for community purposes is outrageous.

A few preliminary notes about the proceedings:

The first is that the Council have failed to produce conclusive evidence of ownership – they still haven't produced the title deeds which seem to have gone on a walkabout somewhere – despite several requests on this matter from campaigners and from those who are in possession of the building.

The second is that the Council hadn't (until yesterday) actually explicitly asked for vacant possession.

And the third is that the Council have impliedly accepted the presence of the occupiers by meeting with the occupiers on the premises.

These points are in tension with the Council's claim that the individuals on the premises are trespassers. It's clear the Council will now only consider an outright purchase of the premises by the community and is not willing to discuss any alternative options.

It's amusing that the Council is seeking to sell property, and is relying upon this point to seek vacant possession when it has so far been unable to produce the conclusive proof it has ownership (the title deeds).

The hearing of the London Borough of Barnet's claim for possession commenced on the 17th December at 10.30 and ran for a full day before a packed courtroom. Some of the defendants are from the Occupy movement. One defendant was a resident and a long-term community activist and joined his name to the defence – Mr. Keith Martin.

The barrister who very kindly agreed to represent the defendants was Ms. Sarah Sackman of Francis Taylor Building; also a former

Barnet resident. The solicitors who were instructed were Leigh Day & Co – with Richard Stein leading.

It was clear that prior to the occupation, there had been an on-going protest and campaign against the closure of the library.

On the 15th June 2012, Maria Persak-Enefer, a local architect, had applied to have the building listed as a community asset pursuant to the Localism Act 2011. This application was not accepted by the local authority until 2nd December 2012, after Leigh Day & Co wrote a pre-action protocol letter threatening judicial review and listing the failure to determine this application as one of the grounds for judicial review.

In making their first legal point, the defendants relied upon the communications between the Council and the occupiers up until this point, and upon the fact that no official had explicitly asked for possession of the premises up until the point of issuing possession proceedings to argue for an implied licence (as opposed to unlawful trespass) on the property. The judge concluded that there was no implied licence; as the failure to ask for vacant possession or to use the term 'trespasser' was not in and of itself a grant of a licence. The judge also stated that, as a licence was a contract, this would require the existence of a legal entity, person or groups a licence was granted to, and that upon the face of the minutes it was clear that council officials had no authority to licence the occupiers to remain on the premises.

The argument that there was an implied licence therefore failed – it was concluded that the occupiers were on the land unlawfully.

A second point was raised by Ms. Sackman on behalf of the defence. During the course of these negotiations the occupants inside the library had essentially re-opened the library, running it as, naming and labelling it the 'People's Library'. The response from the local community was as quick as it was remarkable – over 8,000 books were donated, to the effect that the library had more books than the original Council library had.

Community members operated a volunteer-run rota, and offered free assistance and community services. As a result numerous classes were run on an almost-daily basis between Tuesdays and Sundays from October up until the hearing. These classes included creative writing, belly-dancing, pilates, yoga, comic book classes, French and chemistry. There had been a Cabaret evening, open mic nights and rock gigs inside the library. There had also been regular community campaign meetings – including meetings of the Save Friern Barnet Library inside the building, and there had been a book signing with renowned author Will Self, as well as a campaign day focusing on highlighting broader cuts to public services including the attendance of the leader of the Green Party and key individuals from UNISON.

The nature, manner, and form of this protest – namely, the running of the occupied library itself – as a library – was eloquently argued by Ms. Sackman to be the exercise of the right to protest against the cut to that specific library. It was argued that this right was interfered with, and therefore engaged.

That is to say – the very act of taking over an empty building which once was formerly a library in order to run it as a library – to show that there was still a need for the community library – was the exercise of the community's right to freedom of expression, and of its right to assemble and associate in a protest against the closure of that library. These two rights are enshrined in the Human Rights Act 1998 (Article 10, and Article 11).

This argument was accepted by the judge – who accepted that both the rights to freedom of expression, and the right to assemble and associate had been interfered with by the Council. She recognised that the occupation formed a part of a pattern of protests long before the occupation of the library itself, including the pop up libraries situated on the green beside the library. She also recognised the significant publicity that the campaign had gained both nationally and internationally.

The judge recognised that the defendants had not, as was ruled in the case relating to the occupation of St. Paul's churchyard (*City of London v Samede, 2012),* stopped individuals from worshipping. Neither had they breached the peace. They had in fact been a welcome addition to the local community, and had gained the trust of local businesses. There had been no complaints made about the restriction of local trade – and indeed the occupiers had engaged in positive activity with the local community and business.

This meant that the Council had to demonstrate that this interference was necessary, proportionate and the least restrictive measure available in the circumstances) in order to justify its decision to seek that possession order.

Ms. Sackman had argued that the Council was required to seek the least restrictive measures of interfering with the Art 10 and Art 11 rights which had been engaged. She argued that the least restrictive measures would have been granting a licence to the occupiers to remain on the premises until the building had been sold at the end of the 18 month period provided for by the Localism Act 2011; as opposed to pursuing a possession order.

The community had heard on the 2nd December 2012 that the application for local listing of the community library had been finally determined – and that the Council building had been listed as a community asset under the Localism Act 2011. This essentially meant that when the Council marketed the building a community group could put in an expression of interest for a bid, and then use a period of six months to formulate and submit a bid. Under the present regulations, the Council would be prohibited from selling the building for 18 months from the point at which that expression of interest had been put in.

Ms. Sackman therefore argued that the least restrictive measures would have been granting a licence to the occupiers to remain on the premises until the building had been sold at the end of the 18 month period provided for by the Localism Act 2011 legislation; and not pursuing a possession order. It had already been adduced in evidence that the occupiers would be willing to leave the premises once they had been allowed to exercise their right to protest during the 18 month period, and once the community bid under the Localism Act 2011 had been considered.

Ms. Sackman also argued that the Council had not provided any substantial reasons for why the Council's interference with these rights to lawful assembly and freedom of expression was proportionate. In this case, the Council had only argued that there would be an infringement of planning and building safety regulations as the occupiers had, by sleeping in the building, turned non-residential premises into residential premises.

However, the judge decided that, upon the facts, the Council's decision to pursue a possession order was a proportionate means of achieving a legitimate aim; on the basis that allowing the occupiers to remain in the building during the 18 month period would be prejudicial to any other alternative community bidders who wished to put in a competitive bid for the asset under the Localism Act 2011. She held that the Council would be exposed to 'justified claims of bias', would render the Council to challenge by judicial review, would put off other community groups if there was no guarantee of vacant possession, and that allowing the occupation to continue would constitute an interference with the lawful right to the application to participate in bidding under the Localism Act 2011. She held also, that once the London Borough of Barnet had obtained vacant possession, it would be easier to allow potential bidders to enter the library.

Finally, the judge concluded that a licence could not have been granted by the London Borough of Barnet to the individuals on the premises as a less restrictive interference with these human rights as

(i) at no stage had the defendants made an offer to enter into a legal licence with the claimants, and (ii) the defendants had not identified who the legal persons to be granted that licence were. Furthermore, at no stage had the defendants named a person who was willing to sign a licence.

It was concluded that
- entry onto the premises, notwithstanding negotiations and the conduct of the council was unlawful and was trespass (and not an implied licence);
- the individuals on the premises' human rights to lawful assembly and association, and to freedom of expression were interfered with by the Council (these rights were 'engaged');
and that
- this interference was proportionate and the least restrictive measure available to the Council in light of the need to maintain an impartial, non-prejudicial sale process for diverse community groups to have an opportunity to bid for the recently listed local community library.

Ms. Sackman's application for permission to appeal was rejected; although there remains the recourse to apply to the Court of Appeal.

In terms of legal outcomes a possession order was granted to the Council, but this will not be enforced until February 2013. The Council provided a legal undertaking to that effect. Furthermore, the judge directed the Council to engage again in discussions with the local community about the running of a community library under a contractual licence. Finally, the community will now, upon the listing of the library as a community asset, be able to put together a bid for the library during a period in which the Council will not be able to sell the property.

It is significant that the library is a listed community asset. The library's status reflects what it always was: a community asset and a community building. Members of the community fought so hard to save the library – both inside the court building as well as outside of it – because what they were fighting for was community, opportunity and education. Or, as young Malala, shot by the Taliban for campaigning for women's education so eloquently put it – for the idea that the 'content of a book holds the power of education'. The content of a library also holds the power of education. That is a vision around which the future of the building should now be built.

To reiterate - I'm passionate about literacy. About books, about writing, and above all, about the potential words have to change the direction of a person's life.

OCCUPATION PHOTOGRAPHS

From LtoR: Keith Martin. Feeding pizzas to people taking part in the first nationwide sit-in at FBL. National Libraries Week march, Friern Barnet 2012

From LtoR: Marching for National Libraries Week 2012. The first Pop-up Protest Library. Hanging the issue/return book sign.

From LtoR: Dorrell Dressekie, Maryla Enefer, Dr Ollie Natelson; The People's Library sign that appeared overnight after closure; Save Friern Barnet Library Group.

From LtoR: Keys that had been left behind making the Occupiers job easier. Occupiers: Phoenix, John & Mr Greenacres, 5th September 2012. Empty shelves inside the library.

From LtoR: Daniel (The Caretaker), Phoenix, Library cat made by Julia Kerrison. Positive vibes around the cherry tree.

From LtoR: Donald Lyven and Lucy Nowell who met and fell in love in the library. Theresa Musgrove. Rosa De Souza and Will Self; Revolution! Pete Phoenix, who climbed through a window, and Mr Greenacres, who opened the library doors.

From LtoR: Will Self talking about libraries. Christmas Day in the library with amongst others Keith Martin, Daniel, Hymn, Frances, John, Tirza and Leon.

From LtoR: Outside the Courthouse Petra, Phoenix & Alfred. Me,
Rosa, Phoenix, Daniel and
Petra. an Occupier reading in Friern Barnet Library.

Cue: Open
Libraries are raucous clubhouses for free speech, controversy and community. Librarians have stood up to governments, sat down with noisy toddlers, and reached out to illiterate adults. Libraries can never be shushed! ...

From LtoR: Charlie Honderick and The Hamptons. sign about libraries

WITNESS STATEMENTS

FIONA BRICKWOOD, PETE PHOENIX, KEITH MARTIN, MR GREENACRES

At the trial on Monday 17th December 2012, Fiona Brickwood (supporter of the defendants and community), Peter Phoenix (defendant from the Occupy movement) and Keith Martin (defendant and resident, who applied to be joined with the defendants) gave evidence before Barnet County Court and Judge Patricia Pearl. Mr Greenacres also made a statement but was not called to give evidence.

Ms. Brickwood:
I, Fiona Brickwood of [*address not disclosed for data protection reasons*] WILL STATE AS FOLLOWS:

I make this statement in support of the defendants to the possession proceedings brought by the Claimant.

Insofar as the facts in this statement are within my knowledge they are true. Insofar as the facts in this statement are not within my direct knowledge, they are true to the best of my knowledge and belief.

I have been a resident in Friern Barnet for sixteen years. I was not actively involved in any political matters until the council planned to dispose of our local library, in 2011.

Losing Friern Barnet Library would be very damaging to our community. It is our only public building, so the only place where community activities can take place. A quarter of the children in our ward live in poverty. It is much harder to shift the cycle of deprivation if there is no local library.

In 2011, Barnet Council conducted a major consultation asking all Barnet residents whether they agreed the council's plans to replace Friern Barnet and North Finchley libraries with a "Landmark Library" to be built in North Finchley. 73% of respondents said they did not agree to this proposal, but the Council decided to disregard the result of their consultation and proceed with their plans to close both libraries.

This created huge public protest, with two petitions presented to Cabinet and many letters to councillors and the press.

The council did not need to cut this service as the £432,000 they budgeted to receive from the sale of the library is only 0.0015% of their annual budget. The social cost to Friern Barnet of losing our library would be high, and the monetary gain to the council from disposing of this asset would be insignificant, so I believe that this plan to dispose of our library is contrary to the public interest.

In July 2011, a group of residents and local businesses, including myself, offered to develop a Neighbourhood Plan, to retain Friern Barnet library, whilst generating money to help the council's financial problems. In response to my question at a cabinet meeting on 26 July 2011, the council agreed to defer closure of the library to allow us time to develop the proposal, and promised to make their officers and resources available to work with us on this (Exhibit 1.1). Since then, our group ("Friern Barnet Co-Action") has continued to work with various senior council officers to develop this proposal.

Friern Barnet Co-Action has had various meetings with council officers to discuss and develop our proposals. The council's deadline for community proposals was extended twice, firstly to 31 December 2011 and then to 31 March 2012.

The Cabinet then decided to close the library in April this year, against the advice of its own Scrutiny Committee. However, the council has continued to work with Friern Barnet Co-Action, to develop our proposal for a Community Hub based in Friern Barnet Library.

I have supported the campaign to save Friern Barnet library since it started in the spring of 2011. After the library was closed – against the wishes of the people and the advice of the council's Scrutiny Committee – I helped the Save Friern Barnet Library group to organise and run a 'pop up' library on the Library Green, (an open space located adjacent to the library building). I stored books, which had been donated to the pop-up library, in my home, delivered and collected them each week, and helped staff the book stalls. This "pop-up" library served several purposes: it demonstrated local opposition to the closure of the library and also showed the need for a library service in the local area.

The local community has been very supportive of the campaign, especially the Royal British Legion, who are located next to the Friern Barnet Library site and who have agreed to be part of our Community Hub and Neighbourhood Plan. They supported the pop-up libraries by lending us tables, storing some books, and providing tea for the library campaign to raise donations.

Having the pop-up library reaffirmed that the library building and the surrounding open space is land which belongs to the community, and it allowed us to assert our right to that. Barnet Council is now seeking a possession order over the open land as well as the land where the library building stands, but it is my belief that the public is entitled to use the open land beside the library building to meet, socialise and demonstrate on, and that we have a right of expression to do so.

Following the pop-up library demonstrations, the library building was occupied on 4 September 2012. At the time, the council was considering our application for a £40,000 grant to support our proposal. This included library facilities in Friern Barnet Library and a community-run Enterprise Hub to help people into work, funded by the profits from an Apprentice Cafe, which our group will run in a local cafe. (We are currently in discussion with the cafe owners.)

Following the occupation and reopening of the library as a library by volunteers, I attended several meetings between council officers, residents and occupiers to negotiate proposals for a library and community hub provision in Friern Barnet.

The first two meetings (10th and 17th September) were in the Friern Barnet Library building; the third meeting was at the Council's offices at North London Business Park; the fourth meeting (which I did not attend) was at the Council's site at South Friern library.

All meetings were with senior council officers. Up to thirty residents attended these meetings, with some of the occupiers including Pete Phoenix, and many long-standing campaigners for the reopening of the library including Keith Martin, Mr Greenacres and Rosie Canning.

We asked officers repeatedly whether the key decision maker for the libraries (Robert Rams) was available to attend the negotiations. The officers had said that they would ask him, but subsequently informed us that he was too busy to attend.

Throughout all these meetings and negotiations, we discussed our proposals to have a library on the Friern Barnet Library site itself. During our meetings, Bill Murphy stated very explicitly that he was required to produce £400,000 for the library budget, and that if this was not provided from the sale of Friern Barnet Library, we would need to produce it in some other way. This is inconsistent with the council's offer in October 2011, where they said they would allow us to run a community-run library in Friern Barnet library, renting the building, provided this was done at 'little or no cost to the council'.

Pete Phoenix discussed with Bill Murphy being given the time to raise the £400,000 to buy back the Friern Barnet library site. The council officers repeatedly offered the option of setting up a community-run library in Friary House.

The council have been offering us Friary House for a community-run library since July 2011. We residents have repeatedly told the council that Friary House is unsuitable for a library, because its location in the park is not fully accessible for people with disabilities, and it would be unsafe to access in the late evenings and the nights.

We also asked whether we were negotiating with the right members of staff, i.e. whether the council officers who were negotiating with us actually had the authority to agree to our retaining Friern Barnet Library. It was confirmed to us that these decisions were in fact not in the remit of those library officers any longer as the building had moved to the remit of the property disposals team. It is not clear to me whether the officers who entered into negotiations with us intended to, or were equipped to make the decisions they needed to make to achieve a constructive solution with the community.

We had been under the impression, during our conversations with the council officers, that there would be no attempt to evict the occupiers and the library volunteers while these negotiations were on-going. We had concluded the second meeting and had made arrangements for the third meeting when the defendants received the notice of possession proceedings. As a result we were in the odd situation of continuing to discuss proposals for the continued use and community provision of the Friern Barnet Library premises whilst they had already issued proceedings against the occupiers.

It remains my belief that as the building and especially the green space around it is land that belongs to the community - the building was given to the council for public health purposes and bought specifically for the purpose of creating a public library - that Barnet Council does not have a right to stop members of the public from using the building for community purposes or from demonstrating inside the building. It is clear that people have donated these books and given their time to the running of the community library because they want this library to remain open. They are protesting against this specific cut in the local area as well as providing a valuable service to community. I believe that it was deeply wrong for the Council to make this cut.

Neither the pop-up libraries on the Library Green nor the volunteer library inside the Friern Barnet Library building have caused any nuisance or disturbance to others. On the contrary, they have provided a valued service to the community in a space specifically adapted to that purpose.

WITNESS STATEMENT

PETE PHOENIX

Mr. Phoenix:

I, Peter Phoenix of *[address not disclosed for data protection reasons]*WILL STATE AS FOLLOWS:

I make this statement in support of my defence to the possession proceedings brought by the Claimant.

Insofar as the facts in this statement are within my knowledge, they are true. Insofar as the facts in this statement are not within my direct knowledge, they are true to the best of my knowledge and belief.

Background information
I am a community activist and a member of the Occupy movement. I had received a phone call from the Occupy movement who stated that they needed my help in relation to this particular occupation. I am known as a specialist in working with community centres, and I have experience in communicating and facilitating dialogue between owners and occupiers – especially in working out interim use agreements between owners and occupiers where there are large empty buildings. For example, I have worked with the Jewish Community Centre for London and successfully negotiated a deal for the community, and have also worked with Circle Anglia Housing Association in negotiating housing provision for the homeless.

One of my reasons for choosing this particular building is because I believe that there remains a need for libraries as beacons of education and learning, and as institutions that provide free access to knowledge. I wanted to draw attention to the social cost of the cuts to local authority budgets, and the effect that would have on individuals. The original occupier of Friern Barnet library, Dave, was once a librarian. He left after the third day of occupation but had initiated this entry into the building as he wished to reopen the library. He knew that there was a large local campaign which had hosted demonstrations outside of the library but felt that this campaign would have a stronger voice if the community could run a community library as a form of protest, and that this occupation would provide the community with a greater platform to express their opposition to this local cut to their local library.

Chronology of Events
I entered the building on the 5th September 2012 after two individuals entered before me from the Occupy movement on the 4th September 2012. I had been let in by them through the back door. The two individuals who entered before me, John and Dave, informed me that on the afternoon of the 4th September 2012, a lady from the Library Services department in Barnet Council called Heather Mills had offered the individuals another building to use. Council officers had visited them and had offered the downstairs room of Friary House, with the potential to use the upstairs rooms for the purposes of establishing and running a community library.

I asked John and Dave to take a note of what had happened. We then emailed the Council to thank them for their kind offer of use of Friary House on 5th September; and asked some questions. These were (1) how many rooms were on offer, and (2) when the move into Friary House could take place. The Council responded by email the day after (6th September 2012) where they clarified that both the upstairs and the downstairs rooms were on offer, and that before a move into the building was effected, a lengthy list of details needed to be supplied.

At this point the Council had at no stage in their discussions with us mentioned anything about our trespassing on Council property, nor did officers ask us to leave. In fact they engaged in extensive negotiations over 4 meetings, discussing financial options to run a community library.

After receiving this email, we called the Council and indicated our interest in the proposal. Heather Wills from the council asked for a meeting with Council officials including Julie Taylor – Assistant Chief Executive, on the following Monday 10th September at 10.00 am on the premises at Friern Barnet Library. Again, at no point at this stage in their discussions did the Council state that we were trespassers.

I then invited members of the community who had been longstanding activists for a community library in the local area to attend this meeting. 28 local residents appeared at this initial meeting, including a number of well-known Barnet bloggers as well as, Keith Martin and Fiona Brickwood, all of whom have also provided their witness statements.

This meeting lasted around an hour, and I undertook to facilitate this meeting between these members of the community and the Council. There was significant anger towards council officials –

primarily focused upon the fact that the Council had only agreed to consult and discuss the issue of library provision with members of the community after the occupation had happened, and had failed to enter into constructive negotiations with the community before this event. They had also ignored the response to the Library consultation where 73% of the replies said they wanted to save this library and not have the Arts Depot Landmark Library project, which has since been cancelled.

We had still not been told at this stage that we were trespassing on the property, (in fact at none of the 4 council community liaison meetings were we told that we were trespassing nor were we asked by Barnet Council to leave the building) and the Council agreed to meet with myself, the other occupiers, as well as members of the community a week later on the Friern Barnet Library premises (on 17 September 2012) to discuss proposals for the provision of library services in the local area.

Around this time, myself, Mr Greenacres and Fiona Brickwood were shown around Friary House by Heather Mills (2nd visit of our group). I have attached photos of this extensive guided tour visit where we discussed in detail rooms possible to be used, marked Exhibit 1.1.

There were around 25 members of the community at this second meeting. I continued to facilitate the meeting. At this meeting we agreed to discuss some proposals for library provision which were on the table. We were informed by Mr Cooper from the property services department that the library was not to be used yet for a period of six to eighteen months.

We discussed with the Council the interim use of Friern Barnet library as a community/council run and volunteer run library at low cost. At the third meeting (24.09.2012) with Council officers which was held at Council offices in North London Business Park, seven or eight members of the community were present.

In our discussions with council officers Bill Murphy and Mike Fahey from Library Strategy, a number of proposals were considered which involved Friern Barnet Library.

- *A revenue/rental option*
- *A purchase for £400,000 option*
- *A completely voluntary run library option, with £10,000 and 10,000 books as well as integration into the library computer system.*

Mike Fahey mentioned that the council did options appraisals, so we supplied them with our own options document by the next week outlining 9 possible variable proposals.

Bill Murphy (Library Strategy) stated that if the community could raise an estimated £30,000 – £40,000 of revenue for the rental of Friern Barnet library, that would enable the Council to borrow the £400,000 it needed to keep the library open, and to make up for the identified deficit that the sale of the building was intended to solve.

The Council had offered £10,000, along with 10,000 books to fund a volunteer-run community library. We then emailed the Council and asked them whether the £10,000 offered could be subtracted from the £30-40,000 to reduce the sum that needed to be raised to £20,000-30,000. I then estimated on a rough spread sheet how that revenue of £400-600/week could be generated to enable the library to remain open and provided this estimate to council officers.

This offer was again made by the community and by the occupiers to the Council at the fourth meeting at the South Friern Library building on 10th October 2012. The council officer in question responded that he would have to 'ask whether there is a political will' to accept the proposal where the community raised between £30,000-40,000 for the library to remain open.

Bill Murphy said that the council was very eager to engage with the New Carnegie Foundation who may have been able to raise significant funds to purchase this building and open other Academy Buildings, as they had the backing of several American millionaires.

Bill Murphy said that the council was most interested in Option 4 – the purchase of the building for £ 400,000 and that if we produced this, we could have the building.

We agreed to have a 5th meeting. However, the Council officials noted that meeting the following week would clash with the possession proceedings and the court hearing so they agreed to meet the week after the possession proceedings. Mike Fahey said he would check the availability of the room in South Friern Library for the week after the court case.

This meeting never happened. We feel we were significantly close to finding a mutually beneficial solution for community and council and would like more time to find a resolution. We have made an offer to enter mediation with the help of Berkeley Square professional mediators, but this offer was declined.

The Council's application for a possession order ran completely counter to the fact that the Council had asked us to enter into negotiations about the use of Friern Barnet Library, and had never explicitly told us that we were trespassing on the premises whilst the library was being used and operated as a community library.

In fact, our ability to run the library seemed to form the basis and reason for their on-going discussions and negotiations with us as they saw that there was an opportunity to work with us to provide volunteer-run services at a low cost in order to meet their statutory obligations.

Conclusion

I believe that not only did Barnet Council grant us an implied licence to be on the property while they were commencing possession proceedings, but also that pursuing a possession order itself interferes with the community's right to be on the premises in order to effect a strong protest.

I believe that this is the Council's sole reason for seeking possession and that there is no justification for interfering with this right to community protest and individual expression. The grant of a possession order will interfere with the right to protest.

The level of media coverage and the platform that this occupation has given individuals has meant that the community and community groups have support that they would not otherwise have had. They have been covered in national media; such as the Guardian, the Independent and the Daily Mirror, BBC, ITV and have received significant attention on television and radio (including German television, and French/Swedish radio).

It has enabled the community to express their support for the library through donating over 8000 books, as well as volunteering to fill in a community librarian's rota and through using the library. The location of the occupation of Friern Barnet Library and the way in which the community has registered its protest against the library closure by operating the library is critical to the message we wish to send to the Council. There have many very well attended community talks, workshops and discussions in the library building.

It has also enabled the community to provide a library service to themselves – something that is currently not being provided as a consequence of the closure of Friern Barnet Library. The operation of the library is not causing any nuisance or interference to others.

We have also recently heard that the proposals for a substitute library at the Arts Depot in Finchley have been shelved, which has implications for the Council's statutory duty to provide an efficient and comprehensive library service under the Museums and Libraries Act 1964.

We are, in effect - through running a community library – stepping in to make up for the Council's failure to meet its statutory obligations.

WITNESS STATEMENT

KEITH MARTIN

Mr. Martin:

I, Keith Martin of *[address not disclosed for data protection reasons]*
WILL STATE AS FOLLOWS:

I make this statement in support of my defence to the possession proceedings brought by the Claimant.

Insofar as the facts in this statement are within my knowledge they are true. Insofar as the facts in this statement are not within my direct knowledge, they are true to the best of my knowledge and belief.

I have been a long-standing campaigner for the reopening of, and against the closure of Friern Barnet Library. I participated in both the pop up demonstrations and in the sit in at the Friern Barnet Library which had been hosted by the local Save Friern Barnet Library Campaign Group. Both the consultation and the wider library strategy showed how unpopular the closure of the local library was – as did the continued campaign against its closure, and the campaign to reopen the library. By protesting on the grass beside the library building, the community continuously demonstrated that it had a point to make and that it would continue to use public land in order to make that point. Furthermore, by protesting inside the building by using what was once an empty disused space to run a community library, the community has also demonstrated that it had a point to make against this cut to the library service. It has done so by contributing, volunteering for, and donating to the on-going running of the library service.

It is my understanding that this library was given to the people of Friern Barnet with the support of the Carnegie Foundation. The Carnegie Foundation donated money for the provision of library services in the local area. I believe that Barnet Council have no right to close the library, and that the people of Friern Barnet have the right for the site to be continued to be used for community purposes and as a library.

I attended three out of the four negotiations which took place. These were mainly chaired by the lead occupant Pete Phoenix. I believe that Pete Phoenix has great ability to enable effective dialogue to take place between the Council and the community. We had asked him if he would be willing to facilitate these discussions and he said he would be happy to do so.

I attended both of the negotiations at Friern Barnet Library itself. I also attended the fourth negotiation at the South Friern Library premises. I can confirm that Rosie Canning, another long-standing activist, was there and took detailed minutes of the first two meetings which are a permanent record of the discussions between Council officers and the team who were negotiating on behalf of the community. Roger Tichborne took minutes of the fourth meeting. These negotiations included myself, Peter Phoenix who is the main occupant of the library, Rosie Canning, Fiona Brickwood, Mr Greenacres, and some local bloggers – such as Roger Tichborne who runs a blog called 'The Barnet Eye', and Theresa Musgrove, who runs a blog under the alias of 'Mrs Angry'. After the second meeting, some of us met with council officers at Friern Barnet Library and travelled to Friary House for a viewing of the site. This was offered to us in exchange for the occupiers ceasing the occupation. We declined the site for several reasons. One was that it was not accessible as it was in a dark and unlit area. Another was that we knew that it had been intended to be rented to the police and was a building designed for police and not library use. We also knew that there were some South Asian community groups within the building (which is used at an almost maximum capacity) and we were not clear where they would go, or when a library would be available on those premises.

The first meeting at Friern Barnet Library did not rule out the possibility that the community library would continue to run on the premises with the consent of the Council. There were several options that were on the table – and one suggestion provided by Julie Taylor, who is the Assistant Chief Executive of Barnet Council, was the site at Friary House. Phoenix accepted that this was a possible option. However, Friern Barnet Library ruled out.

At the first meeting the local blogger Roger Tichborne asked Craig Cooper (a representative from the Property/Estates department at Barnet Council) whether the building remained within the remit of Cllr Robert Rams. He responded that it was 'no longer a library, it was an asset'. It is my belief that Barnet Council were not genuinely interested in negotiating to keep the library open. When the occupiers learnt that a possession order would be sought and that papers had been filed for eviction, this came as a complete surprise as we had agreed to continue negotiating. This behaviour was completely at odds with the dialogue and mediation which had been taking place between council officers and residents/occupiers at the meetings about the provision of library services. I did not feel that this was the act of an honest negotiator.

I believe also that council officers made statements implying a promise not to issue proceedings. Julie Taylor had promised to convey to councillors the views of those who met that negotiations should be continued between the council and the community. She had said 'I can guarantee you, that I will put that point of view to the councillors.' It had also been stated that 'no snap decisions would be made', when local blogger Theresa Musgrove asked as to whether the Council would be seeking possession.

There was therefore an implication here that the Council would not torpedo negotiations by applying for a possession order or eviction proceedings, especially as the main occupant (Pete Phoenix) was by this point recognized as essential to facilitating the negotiations by both sides. The council then continued to offer to meet with the community group and with the occupants including myself to negotiate for the provision of library services after the papers for possession had been issued. Negotiations have now ceased.

I am, as well as a witness, a defendant. I wanted to add my name to the list of defendants as I wished Barnet Council to know that their action was not simply against non-residents of Barnet but also against long standing residents and the council taxpayer. I have supported this occupation and have joined my name as a co-defendant to this action because I wish to refute any suggestion that the defendants comprise of non-residents only, to refute the suggestion that the Council is merely taking action against individuals, rather than the community. I join my name to the defendants on behalf of the local community as a long standing activist.

The local community want this library to be reopened, and have continuously been protesting against its closure through the act of using the library itself, donating to the library and volunteering to run the community library.

WITNESS STATEMENT

MR GREENACRES

Mr. Greenacres:

I, Mr Greenacres of *[address not disclosed for data protection reasons]* WILL STATE AS FOLLOWS:

I make this statement in support of my defence to the possession proceedings brought by the Claimant.

Insofar as the facts in this statement are within my knowledge, they are true. Insofar as the facts in this statement are not within my direct knowledge, they are true to the best of my knowledge and belief.

About Myself

My name is Mr Greenacres, I am 57 years old and have lived in the area my whole life. I am an experienced master carpenter and builder and I am also very knowledgeable in local green spaces which I have a strong interest in. I host slide shows at various venues in the borough where I present photographs of green spaces, water features and other areas of community interest within the borough. I am a member of and hold various positions in several prominent local societies and community groups. I have been raising awareness of and campaigning for local green spaces and heritage buildings for over 35 years.

Friern Barnet Library

Friern Barnet Library is a charming 1934 period municipal built library. I believe it is of high architectural merit and is noteworthy for its wide expanse of windows on all sides of the building creating something of an art studio feel in terms of light. I understand there is a local listing application pending. Many of the period features are intact and well preserved including interior and exterior oak panelled doors. I have supported the campaign to keep this library open from the very minute I heard of Barnet Council's intention to close it. I think it is quite wrong to close this building and it is my belief that Barnet Council is failing in its statutory duty to provide library services to the people who live in Friern Barnet.

Entry to the library building

I heard on the 5th September that the library had been 'occupied'. I was in the area, so I went to the premises to see what was happening. I met two occupiers and I immediately offered my support because I believed what they were doing was morally right. They had gained access through a hinged rear window. At the point I arrived, the doors were not open. We discussed getting the doors open and I said the easiest thing would be if we could find the keys. One of the occupiers, who was inside said, "there's loads of keys in here". We subsequently found that every key to  every lock in the building had been left inside the building. Once the doors were open, I entered and made an inspection of the premises and can report the following:

Firstly, THERE WAS ABSOLUTELY NO FORCED ENTRY INTO THIS BUILDING. I note that Suzanna Lewis has stated, in her statement, *'They appear to have gained access by unfastening a window and knocking away a timber security bar which would have required the use of tools to do so.'*

The windows in this building are metal framed and of original 1934 construction, the inward-opening frames are fastened shut with spring-loaded fanlight catches which have a protruding ring-pull. They are operated from ground level by a boat hook on a wooden pole. Quite simply, two windows do not fasten properly and in my professional opinion have not done so for quite a while, they are congealed with excess paint and no longer align to the striking plates/mortises. Suzanna Lewis's reference to *'knocking away a timber security bar'*, is also misleading. Bits of 21x45mm timber batons were wedged between the bottom of the catch and a ledge below, this is a makeshift job and in the case of the two windows that do no fasten properly, the batons would simply have fallen away and would not require the use of tools which is pure supposition on the part of Ms Lewis.

Ms Lewis also states, *'I believe that the occupants are using the utilities too and have also caused other damage to the premises, including the back door.'* No doors were forcibly entered into or damaged. I have photographic evidence of this as I took photographs the day we entered the building. I have also included a photograph with a dated newspaper on the outside of the back door which shows that the doors were intact and in good condition after the 6th September 2012.

The allegation that occupiers have caused other damage to the premises cannot be further from the truth. The occupiers and various community members have cleaned, polished and reassembled book shelves, cleaned windows, thoroughly hoovered and cleaned the building at regular intervals, fixed the toilet cistern, swept the yard and cleared rubbish from the building and generally kept the building in good order. I myself have carried out health and safety checks and made sure that all the doors and fire escapes are in good working order.

Burglar Alarm - Blue 9 Security Statement

On the 6th September, I was present at the library with Pete Phoenix. We were approached by a security guard calling to us in a not unfriendly manner over the fence. He said the alarm was going off somewhere, it was not very clear to us where it was going off as it had been switched off for several days. But, he said he wanted to come in and disarm the panel inside the building. This was a fairly friendly exchange and we said he could come in and inspect the panel on the condition that he did not take any photographs or remove anything from the building. He went straight to the burglar alarm key-pad panel and very quickly appeared to have removed it from the wall. He then said he wanted to remove it from the building. We said, we didn't want him to remove anything from the building as we may be held liable for it. I subsequently learnt his name was, Lukasz Ciupina and have read his statement which contains the sentence: *'the door lock being smashed'*. I cannot understand how a professional security guard could have got it so wrong, the door lock was not 'smashed'. This is a false allegation.

Community use of the building

Since the occupation, a community library has been set up in a very competent and professional manner. Strength of feeling within the local community is clearly indicated by the fact that the following have been donated by local individuals, businesses and schools:

Some 8,000 books, numerous toys, CDs, DVDs and videos, various pieces of furniture including, 6 work tables, 40 stacking chairs, easy chairs, sofas and coffee tables and three working computers and printers. Further to this, a new working fridge has been installed in the kitchen to replace the existing faulty one. I was personally involved in organising and collecting donations of tables and chairs.

 The photo shows the interior of the building in the first few days of occupation. I believe that this level of support allows the community to express their opposition to the cut to library service. The very fact that it is being run as a functioning library by local volunteers is evidence that the Council is interfering with the community's right to object to these closures and the right to use the library.

I believe that the community library initiative and the public support given to it allow the community to express their opposition to the cut in the public library service. The Council has not supported this community initiative; they have sent memos to local schools saying it is not a council run service and urging them not to use it.

They wish to close this community service at the earliest opportunity and their stated intention is only to gain possession of the building and board it up, and thus the Council are interfering with the community's right to object to these closures and their right to use the library.

The Roof

From the very start of the occupation round the clock security guards were posted outside the library 24 hours a day. The guards kept a fairly low profile and were not unfriendly if approached: they were there simply to monitor the situation. After about a week many people, notably local councillors and bloggers, began to raise the issue of the mounting costs of this pointless exercise and realised that the operation was costing about £4600 per week. Surely, an absolute absurdity to spend this much money to keep watch on a closed public building when it costs less than £2000 per week to keep the same building open and running as a library. After ten days, before the scandal of the security costs became too great, the guards were removed from their duties outside the library. On or around the 19th September, three days after the guards were removed, I received a phone call from Daniel Gardonyi, one of the library occupiers. He was quite agitated and was telling me that water was "pouring into the building". At the time I thought he was exaggerating and I told him I would look at the roof the following day. When I got on to the roof the next day, I could not believe what I saw. At the back of the building there is a parapet wall with a rainwater run off gully running the entire length of the rear of the building (this would be in place of the more usual exterior guttering.). At some point in the previous three days, a person or persons unknown had got on to the rear of the roof and caused serious deliberate damage. Now, I have no idea who these perpetrators are but I can report the following:

1) The motive of theft can be ruled out because no materials were actually removed from the roof.

In the photo one can clearly see a large piece of lead that, although easy to carry away, had been left there. There was much deliberate damage and no attempt to remove recyclable valuable materials. In my professional opinion theft was not the motive here.

2) Whoever went up on that roof knew what they were doing. This was not the work of amateurs or mindless vandals. The intention appears to have been to cause as much damage to the roof, threaten the integrity of the building and cause rainwater to enter the building. On the corner as shown, the damage is consistent with a well-aimed kick with the heel of a boot, and this would not be helpful to a thief as it would put smashed tiles and debris all over the valuable lead and zinc.

3) The timing of the incident also very odd. The building had been shut and empty for five months before occupation, and the damage occurred a matter of days after the guards had been pulled off.

As I have said I have no idea who the perpetrators of this wanton vandalism may have been, but in my professional opinion it is not the work of thieves. It is more likely to be someone who has a vested interest in the redevelopment of the building. I immediately supervised the starting of repair works. The debris was cleared, salvageable tiles saved, and repairs were started. Unfortunately through ill health I was unable to supervise the work to completion, but the work has now been completed by roofing contractors and the building is now water tight.

Community Library Operations and Events

Since September 5th, many events have taken place. I was the first person to stage a public event in this new community library. On Saturday September 8th, I ran a *Thunderbirds are Go* presentation for children and a *Waterways of Finchley* slideshow for adults which was a great success.

Since then many events have been staged, including: lectures and tutoring sessions; poetry readings; local history presentations; children's story time; yoga and pilates classes; bicycle maintenance workshops; film shows; discussion groups; creative writing workshops; arts and crafts workshops; musical evenings; even a literary festival. This fantastic array of events has gone far beyond anything that happened in the old library, and I believe this initiative should be encouraged by Barnet Council and not stamped on.

Negotiations with Barnet Council

Senior council officers approached the occupiers on day one with a view to negotiating. Council officers took Pete Phoenix to view Friary House in Friary Park with a view to setting up a community library there, but as it soon transpired this was the one and only thing Barnet Council were willing to negotiate about. Meetings were then set up inside Friern Barnet Library attended by senior council officers, occupiers and various members of the community. These meetings were fully minuted. I attended the first three of these meetings. It quickly became apparent that the council officers showed no real goodwill or intent to negotiate with the community about the reopening of Friern Barnet Library. Although the officers made attempts to appear amenable, they were not forthcoming and little progress was made. For example, when I requested accounts for the last financial year, I was given an incomplete set of figures. I then requested proper accounts and was told there were no proper audited accounts for Friern Barnet Library. I received another set of figures that were completely different from the first set and I have ended up with three completely different sets of figures for the same financial year. Also there was a level of subterfuge and lack of transparency from the officers. For example, one resident, Theresa Musgrove, expressed the query of many when she asked the officers, would they start legal proceedings against the occupiers. Julie Taylor, Deputy Chief Executive, replied that they were in no hurry to start proceedings and that 'we're not making any snap decisions'. I later found out that legal proceedings had been started some days previously. Officers then changed times and venues of meetings and became more controlling and less conducive. They would only negotiate the issue of setting up a library in Friary House which was unanimously unacceptable within the community for a whole range of reasons that I will not go into here.

I stopped attending negotiation meetings after the first three because I saw little productivity in it. What I did try and do was enter into one-to-one negotiations with Cllr Richard Cornelius, Leader of the Council; Cllr Robert Rams, Cabinet Member for Customer Services; and Bill Murphy, Assistant Director Customer Services. I was unable to meet with Cllr Cornelius as he was away, but I had phone conversations with Bill Murphy and Robert Rams and can report the following:

Bill Murphy was unwilling to discuss anything with me, saying, 'I'm not in negotiations with anybody', and 'I'm not discussing anything. It's a legal matter only; it's in the hands of property services.' He did tell me that when he gained possession of the building, it would be 'sealed and secured' and added, 'the only thing we're interested in, as we said all along, is to secure the building and market it for £400,000'. When I tried to raise the issue that maybe the local community would take over the building, he said, 'You can't expect me to comment on that', and with that our conversation ended.

I had a longer conversation with Robert Rams (about 35mins) and whilst his tone was polite with me I was unable to negotiate anything at all. I invited him to visit the library and he declined. I tried to apprise him of the events at the community library and he wasn't interested. He was only interested in vacant possession of the Friern Barnet Library and setting up a community library in rooms in Friary House. He told me he quite liked the occupiers, because he was of the opinion that they had a genuine desire to set up a community library within Friary House. He tried to persuade me to endorse the idea of moving the library to Friary House, even going so far as to offer me money. This was how he phrased it, 'we can give you money', I was quite shocked at the way he put it, he did not say you can apply for grant funding or anything like that, he offered me money. I tried to put the case for keeping the library where it was, a purpose-made building in the right location, but he wasn't interested. I tried to reason with him that, as there was going to be some delay in handing the building to a developer, what would be the harm of running a community library in the interim period. He was reluctant to answer this point, which I asked several times. He merely said, 'It's our political will to close this building and have it redeveloped'. I even tried to negotiate that in the event Barnet Council were given possession of the building, a reasonable time period be given for the winding down of the community library. Robert Rams thought it reasonable to grant me 24hours, saying it would take half a day to remove things from the library. When pushed, he said, 'Alright, I'll give you a day and a half'. I was shocked at this brutal stance. Barnet Council is hell bent on bulldozing this building; they are not interested in negotiating the community use of this building. They have even sent a contractor into the volunteer run community library to measure up for shutters and boarding. I believe that Barnet Council has failed in its statutory duty to provide library services to the people of Friern Barnet and has failed to properly engage and consider the initiatives of the local community as laid out in the Localism Bill. The decision to close this library was not sound, the Council's own Scrutiny Committee had reservations and it remains the political will of one cabinet member acting on delegated powers. No regard whatsoever has been shown for the history, heritage and welfare of the people of Friern Barnet and no attempt has been made to take an interest in the setting up of a community library on this site.

I would urge this court if in any way possible, not to grant possession of the library building to Barnet Council. It is a public building, owned by the Mayor and Burgesses of the borough. Council Officers have only one stated intention, namely, to seal and secure the building and turn it over to developers. The occupiers and the community on the other hand wish to preserve and regenerate this piece of Friern Barnet Heritage for the local community and have already proved they can do so in a competent manner that is of benefit to the local community. I therefore believe that the local community has demonstrated they have a stronger right to this property than Council Officers.

   If this is not the case, I hope that the Council's claim for a possession order will be struck out on the grounds that:
- there is no urgency around the possession of the building
- the building is being used in the public interest
- the community's right to expression and opposition to this library cut is being interfered with by the Council by getting this possession order; and the Council have no justification for interfering with it.

CHRISTMAS DAY IN THE LIBRARY

FRANCES BRIERS

When I woke up on Christmas Day 2012, it was pouring with rain. We had arranged to walk the dog around Trent Park with our friends, which is what we traditionally do. I was also looking forward to going to the library which was going to be open on Christmas Day. I never thought this was going to happen, because I thought the squatters would be evicted after the court case on 18th December.

About a week before the court case, I went to see Kate Sallinger, Deputy Mayor, at the North Middlesex Golf Club. If the decision went against us in court, we wanted to try and stop the eviction taking place before Christmas. Though Kate felt sure there wouldn't be an eviction before Christmas, she couldn't guarantee it and she did say she had a spare bedroom. I was concerned about Hymn being put out in the cold in the worst winter we'd had for years, because he didn't have anywhere to go. So I was very pleased that the judge also felt that it was too cold for the Occupiers to be evicted before February.

My husband Bob arrived at Trent Park at 9am. It was freezing cold and pouring with rain so he stayed in the car because he was unwell. There were about ten of us on the dog walk and we were gone for about an hour. When we got back, we got our food out of our cars and had our traditional doggy brunch of crackers, cheese, port, bucks fizz and champagne. Then we drove home to dry off and I left Bob indoors whilst I went to the library.

Walking through the doors, I saw Keith Martin who looked like Father Christmas with his white beard. The library was decorated and it smelt Christmassy as incense was burning. Barry Rawlings was there, along with Daniel, Mark, Hymn, Dave and a few others. Lucy and Donald came about fifteen minutes later and then Tirza and Ron arrived with a Persian dish and salad which we tucked into. We had Bucks Fizz, Baileys, champagne and port to drink and had our photographs taken by Lucy.

It was strange to be in the library; in fact it was strange to be in *any* library on Christmas Day. Looking around at all the books, I remembered back to the start of the campaign which had begun at the end of May 2012. The previous year, we had all sat on the floor reading our books and refusing to leave. I decided to join the campaign to help save Friern Barnet Library. It has been a hard fought battle with the council to try and stop them from closing our library, with petitions, people attending council meetings, asking questions, doing research about historical and legal points, holding events in the library and on the village green and meeting lots of lovely people.

I joined the group because it was the last public building in Friern Barnet. The town hall has been turned into flats, The Orange Tree pub reopened as a supermarket and the Duck and Carrot pub is now an Italian Restaurant. For me to get to any other library would have entailed a bus ride and would have meant leaving Bob, who has cancer, on his own for too long. So having a local library, which I could walk to, was very important. When it closed I was very sad. Every day I walked past the empty building with my dogs and think what a waste. SFBL were having regular meetings at the British Legion and collecting signatures for the petition to reopen the library.

After the library closed in April 2012, we held events on the green, including the pop-up library and a jubilee party on Sunday 3rd June, which was also my birthday, and it poured with rain again. Deputy Mayor Kate Sallinger cut the cake, music played despite the rain and we had hot drinks from the Royal British Legion. The Legion had always supported us, letting us use an upstairs room for our meetings and supplying drinks at our events.

During the summer of 2012 we still had hope of reopening the library as it hadn't been sold yet, but no one dreamt of it being occupied by Occupy London. I first heard about the occupation on Twitter and Facebook. Coming back from the shops I did see someone climbing the fence round the back. The following day we were having a meeting in the British Legion; some of our group had spoken to the squatters through the fence who had said they were willing to reopen the library. This excited me a lot. Suddenly a guy with blond dreadlocks came into the meeting with Mr Greenacres and Rosie. Mrs Angry, Dan the Bugle and journalist Chris Hewitt were already there. The guy with the dreadlocks said his name was Phoenix and somebody said, was it Felix? And Phoenix said no, Phoenix, like the bird rising from its own ashes. I never imagined on that day of the meeting, that three months later I would be sitting in the library on Christmas Day eating and drinking, which of course we weren't allowed to do before!

We pulled our crackers and wore our hats and it still felt very surreal. Someone asked if I could help him with his penalty benefit notice.

'You're lucky as our local councillor is here.'

Barry said, "I'm not working Christmas day." But he did have a look and advised the gentleman. I asked Mark and Hymn if they still wanted a traditional Christmas lunch (a vegetarian one). They said yes and I told them I would go home, cook it and come back later.

I got home, prepared Bob's dinner and mine, and cooked extra for the guys in the library. I got the big picnic basket down and all sorts of ice cream containers to try and keep everything hot. Luckily I don't live far from the library; I was able to cover everything with a tea-towel and take it round, still warm. The table was still set with odd bits of food so I called in the occupiers who were outside having a smoke, and they had their second Christmas meal: roast potatoes, roast parsnips, broccoli, sage and onion stuffing, carrots and no meat. By this time it was getting dark and the library looked very pretty with the Christmas lights all around the desk and on the Christmas tree. And it was lovely to leave the guys listening to music and being so very merry.

COUNCIL STATEMENT

LONDON BOROUGH OF BARNET

This statement was read out by Bill Murphy at the occupied Friern Barnet Library, 10th January 2012:

Following the recent decision of the courts to grant vacant possession of the site, the council would like to make clear it's [sic] view as to the next steps it is seeking to come to a resolution in terms of the future of the building.

This statement will provide clarification in relation to:
1) Disposal of the Building;
2) Regaining vacant possession of the building – the eviction proceedings;
3) Supporting the local community to purchase/lease the building;
4) Intermediate use of the building while disposal process is taking place.

1) **Disposal of the building** – it is proposed that we take a report to Cabinet Resources Committee on 26/2/13 to formally market the building. The Community Right to bid process (CR2B) cannot start until we have done this. Immediately after this meeting we would update the website and send marketing materials to community groups and normal private sector organisations. Under the CR2B - community groups then have 6 weeks to prepare an 'expression of interest'. After a further 4.5 months (total from starting marketing to decision must be at least 6 months) members would consider the bids and make a decision. This would be based on a full understanding of the competing option and real information on the market value of the site. It may well be that other community groups will present bids. The council may make any number of decisions from selling to the highest bidder to agreeing some deal with a local organisation for less than market value. The council could decide to offer the building on

a lease basis. The marketing material will make it clear that we are willing to consider such options. The improved financial position as a result of the NSCSO allows us some flexibility as to how we dispose of the building.

2) **Regaining vacant possession of the building** – the eviction proceedings – Officers have started preparations for eviction proceedings so that we are ready to take action of 1/2/2013. This will involve instructing bailiffs etc. If this is delayed as a result of an appeals process, the council will seek to fully recover its costs. In any event, we can not progress any options until such time as we have vacant possession. Any appeal process could prolong this.

3) **Supporting the local community to purchase/lease the building** – we have asked Community Barnet to work with local residents to assist in forming a 'legal' entity which is able to bid for funds and take on the responsibilities of a properly constituted group. A council officer will provide regular updates on progress. We are clear that the group should consist of local residents and potentially ward councillors. Community Barnet will be available to support a group in preparing a bid to CLG for funding to purchase the building when it has been formally marketed as well as other options, such as leasing, in the event that such a bid is not successful. However, the council does need to make clear that as part of the CR2B process, other organisations may also decide they wish to present alternative options and the council would be bound to support and consider these as well.

4**) Intermediate use of the building while disposal process is taking place** – Once the council has vacant possession, for an initial period, the council will offer a resource to support the continued use of the building for volunteer supported activities. This would require us to negotiate a 'contracted-out-lease' for the period which would enable us to set conditions on the use of the building during this time and be clear about what happens at the end of the period. The resource would be for a 'caretaker +' service that would ensure that activities complied with the terms of the lease (e.g. compliance with CRB checks, planning & building control conditions, Health & Safety etc.)

Bill Murphy, Assistant Director – Customer Services
Barnet Council
10/1/13

THE COUNCIL'S POSITION HAS CHANGED

FROM THERESA MUSGROVE'S BLOG – BROKEN BARNET

Thursday 10th January 2012: A meeting took place last night at the occupied Friern Barnet Library: the People's Library, as it has become, since it was reclaimed for the community by a team of occupiers, and reopened by residents in defiance of the council's determination to sell the property for development.

Bill Murphy, Barnet's Assistant Director of Customer Services, the senior officer with responsibility for libraries was clearly uncomfortable and tried to overcome his sense of discomfort at sitting in a squat, in front of a tent, surrounded by a circle of community activists, and visibly failed.

He struggled on to explain the council's position on the current developments, and to try to undo the damage caused by Tory Cabinet member Robert Rams's contradictory remarks regarding the occupation in statements to the local press - and in his own press release. Rams, in fact, has thankfully fallen silent, or perhaps been gagged - and an officer has had to step in to try and take back control of yet another One Barnet cock up.

It has been confirmed by Bill Murphy that Rams's reported comments in the press this week, suggesting that a local charity would be running the library, and deciding on the granting of a licence is, as the charity, commUNITY Barnet, had already stated, a load of nonsense.

Quite how Rams expects to continue in his role as Cabinet member, in the circumstances, is really rather mystifying, but then we must never underestimate the ability of Barnet Tory councillors to do the wrong thing at the wrong time, and expect to get away with it.

And here is a major admission from the London Borough of Broken Barnet, as announced not by any Tory councillor, of course, but by interim consultant Mr Murphy:

'The council's position has changed'.

In fact, Mr Murphy goes on to say the council's position has 'shifted significantly'. Really? Why so, Mrs Angry wonders?

Could it be that at last, this Tory council, donkeys led by donkeys, has blundered into a muddy field with no way out other than the road to the electoral abattoir, and caught the scent of blood in the air?

Possibly. That's if you believe that Mr Murphy is speaking with authority, and is able to guarantee what the council's position will be once - if - they regain vacant possession of the building, and after the required period of consideration of community proposals for the use of the property is over.

Mrs Angry has read a copy of the Council's statement - (which begins, incidentally, with a glaring grammatical error: eurgh, really ... it's its, not it's) and this otherwise carefully worded document makes it quite clear that the council's focus is on eviction, and marketing. Any obligation to the consideration of community bids is secondary, and theoretical.

Bill Murphy will not be staying around to see what happens to Friern Barnet library - Mrs Angry understands he is leaving Barnet in a few months. Councillor Robert Rams, on the other hand, will be here to delight us all until May 2014.

Throughout the history of the library campaign, the one constant element of the story has been the utter unreliability of any agreements made, or that appear to have been made. Verbal agreements, agreements made by staff not authorised to negotiate, implied agreements, misunderstandings: all of these factors have ensured that hopes by campaigners - that their reasoning was having some effect turned out to be false.

And this is why the campaign has only had any success when direct action was taken, and the use of occupation of what is, after all, morally at least, a building that already belongs to the community in which it is situated, and not to the Tory councillors who want to sell it for a quick buck.

We are told now that 'there is a bit more flexibility' in terms of the library budget, and that the pressing need for a capital receipt from the sale of the building is not quite so pressing. Not quite. Nice words, carefully chosen. We need facts.

Here are some questions:

How much has now become available?

Is it because of the total collapse of Robert Rams' famous invisible landmark library?

If so is all of the funding set aside for this project now available?

What about the substitute landmark library Rams has promised to install instead at the North Finchley branch?

Is the council really prepared to forego the real commercial value of the library in favour of a local community enterprise, leasehold or otherwise?

Is this apparent climb-down an attempt to dampen down the story before the run up to the 2013, elections?

Or is this all another Barnet trick, and are they soft soaping the campaigners into believing that it is safe to end the occupation of the library, leave the premises and hand over the keys to Barnet Council?

It's not just about this building, this borough, or even about the national assault on the public library system: it's about taking a stand, and defending the things you value.

Whatever the outcome - and this story still has a long way to go before it is finished - the fact that the council's position has now 'shifted significantly' is entirely down to the determination, resourcefulness and courage of the people fighting to protect their community.

It is a lesson to others: a lesson for Capita, and any other predatory chancers circling around the boundaries of our borough.

Enter at your own risk: this is Broken Barnet.

Editor's Note:
In fact Bill Murphy did not leave immediately. He went on to implement the Capita programme. The chopping of up to 500 jobs. The editor always thought of him as an axe man, employed like Beeching to rationalise – chop chop chop – and leave, like the railways that were left, with only the minimum of services.

A COUNCILLOR'S VIEW

CLLR BARRY RAWLINGS

November 2009 there were discussions as to what Labour's local pledges would be for Coppetts ward in the 2010 Council elections. One of our main ones was to keep Friern Barnet Library open. The Library Review had not even started but we recognised there would be a threat to this well-loved part of the community.

Soon after the elections, our worst fears came true – the review had recommended the closure of Friern Barnet Library. There were suggestions of a local independent school having the building and Friary House, although totally unsuitable, was being offered as a community facility. It was clear there would be a fight to keep the library. The role of a local councillor meant making it clear where we stood, assisting local people to campaign, ensuring the threat was highlighted in the local press and that it was on the agenda of as many council meetings as possible.

We had previously campaigned to keep South Friern Library open and to save Hollickwood School from closure. Both were successful. The lessons I learned from these campaigns were that they were political, even if not party political. It was about standing alongside the local community, not trying to lead it – being part of the community and not separate from it. In the Council Chamber, Labour Councillors fought the closure but every Conservative councillor voted to close the library so they won the vote. But this was not the end – if anything it galvanised local people to fight harder. Cllr Pauline Coakley-Webb and I attended meetings of the 'Save Friern Barnet Library' group, helped liaise with the local press, produced leaflets and helped with the petition.

I enjoy campaigning: having a common cause brings people closer together. We all learn what skills and talents people have if they are allowed to use them, and it helps transform a neighbourhood into a community. Twice we took the threatened closure to a Scrutiny Committee and both times it was sent back to Cabinet to reconsider their decision. This was vital, not only because it delayed any closure but also because we had convinced some Conservative councillors to follow our lead. It could no longer be defined in party terms but was clearly a wider campaign, which was now involving people of different parties and none. Very important was the support of BAPS, the local press and various bloggers which ensured that we remained centre stage and could not be ignored.

The next phase was the occupation. The 'caretakers' proved a wonderful group of people to work with and without them there may well have been a small supermarket or a small block of flats rather than a marvellous library building. However, it did create difficulties for the Council and through them the councillors. The advice from the legal department was not to enter the buildings while they were being squatted. As Council officers had already started negotiating, Pauline and I decided we should enter and talk to people too. Other Labour Councillors also attended meetings and events, but none of the Conservatives would enter and there was a danger it would become party political and about squatting rather than about community action and saving libraries. Finchley & Golders Green MP Mike Freer had sponsored a bill outlawing squatting in residential buildings after a mansion in Hampstead Garden Suburb had been squatted in, and local Conservative councillors wanted to show their support to Mr Freer.

Importantly BAPS, the local press and Barnet bloggers continued to support the library. The local community recognised Occupy were not taking the building for themselves but opening the doors to all who wanted to use the library. A series of events were organised that brought new people in, such as a book signing by Will Self and the music events. There was international interest - Pauline and I spoke to French and Swedish radio, Chinese television, Japanese papers and the Guardian and Daily Mirror.

Unlike in other authorities the library had not been handed over to the community as part of the Big Society but the community was determined the library would not die so they snatched it back. It gave hope to many other campaigns. We then had to get used to attending the court. Others can explain the legal process and arguments but as a lay person I understood that a judge accepted the Human Rights Act 1998 (Article 10, and Article 11) and that both the rights to freedom of expression, and the right to assemble and associate had been interfered with by the Council. The judge made it clear that she expected the Council to talk to the campaigners – negotiation rather than action by bailiffs was expected.

The negotiations resulted in a two-year lease and a grant of £20,000 for each year. Many of the campaigners feel glad that the library continues but it is only a partial victory as the Council are now no longer responsible for the service. I am sympathetic to this but looking at the campaign up to now leaves me with a question. As a Council service, the costs of the library were paid through taxation, yet a cabinet of ten people, who had never even visited the library, could ignore local people and decide to close the library in a few minutes. It is now run with volunteers but has the opportunity to become a co-operative with local people making the decisions. Which one is better, which one is in reality 'public'?

MASS MOBILISATION

MARTIN RUSSO

When I saw a red banner with the words, 'Save Friern Barnet Library', hanging from the trees opposite the library I began to realise the rumours I'd heard about the closure were true. There were also rumours that there was a public consultation paper and yet, hardly any of us had seen it. That day, I rushed back home and grabbed my camera to take photos of the protest. I had just finished a course in web journalism and thought that it would be a good idea to help, so I used social media to help with the campaign. I set up a website, social networking sites, YouTube, Flickr accounts and sent out the first email for the Save Friern Barnet Library Group on 7th May 2011.

We also started an online petition on Barnet Council's website. A little storm started to gather momentum and by the time of the next Save the Library event, a few dozen people had jumped to hundreds. Something quite remarkable and inspiring was starting to happen. Later, Alan Gibbons joined us along with many celebrated national writers such as Naomi Alderman and Michael Morpurgo. We were later contacted by the BBC to appear on 'The One Show' and it was agreed that I would represent our campaign.

The surrounding area of Friern Barnet has been turning into a place you drive past rather than live in. So holding onto our library was like grabbing the last flicker of public space before the whirlwind of change and development grabbed it and swept it away with the next block of flats or private development.

We wanted to keep the library public and run by the council as a public service. Friern Barnet is a working community, not affluent. We were all hard pushed for time and the prospect of a voluntary-led library fraught with risk was not on our agenda at the time of the SFBLG campaign.

Although we had gained the support of the local community to save the library - the Internet, social networking sites, Twitter, and emails took the plight of the library to a wider community nationally and internationally. We used Twitter on the day of the 'Sit In', April 5th 2012, the day the library closed. *The Guardian*, the BBC and many other major media outlets would have been none the wiser without our tweets from inside the library on that day. This action really helped to attract a small media frenzy and the library was given a good send off before the doors officially closed. I had been at work but after speaking with Hannah Freeman from *The Guardian,* decided to leave early. Hannah asked if I could send in some pictures, video and even audio to upload onto their website, as they wanted to run a live blog.

We amassed a considerable crowd and interest. It was never in the millions but it was enough to mean we were constantly in the local press, and had regular interest from the national media. The committee was at times overwhelmed with the rapid growth of the challenges facing the campaign. It was quite incredible! We were also blessed with a rich array of very active and engaging Barnet bloggers as well as huge support from the local trade union UNISON and Barnet Alliance for Public Services (BAPS).

We used the hashtag #savelibraries that linked us into the national campaign 'Speak Up For Libraries.' Our story did appear to fit neatly into the current narrative of how cuts to public services were affecting communities. We had tapped into something that resonated around the country. We even had copy-cat campaigns spring up across the country. If it was not Philip Pullman saving libraries in Oxfordshire, it was Alan Bennett saving his library in Kensal Green. Our library and the community campaign stood for something greater, we started to symbolise something beyond what many of us could imagine. The campaign demonstrated the power and passion people have for libraries, for reading, and also for benefits afforded from a public space, a library, a community home.

Our petitions eventually reached a staggering seven thousand signatures including Prunella Scales and David Nicholls who supported our cause.

When the Occupy group arrived, they opened up a new chapter for the campaign that lead to a synergy between different groups, including our own, to build and grow in a different form. The opening up of negotiations with Barnet council helped energise our group with a new hope that something really could be achieved. The Occupy group had shown great humility, skill and ability at negotiating, running workshops, organising meetings and building alliances. And finally, there was good news, a new unit would form a group of Trustees along with a community proposal, to create a new community library.

Technology played a huge part in our campaign. It helped our community connect up, engage with a wider network and promoted our neighbourhood community and campaign to the world.

DEMOCRACY IN ACTION

TAMAR ANDRUSIER

Library Under Threat

Friern Barnet Library (FBL) sits next to a village green, near the British Legion and opposite the grand façade of St John's church on Friern Barnet Road. The library is a local landmark and makes a focal point for the area. Take it away and the area would lose its identity and character, becoming just another residential corridor in North London.

Our twins, Oscar and Hannah, were ten years old and in the habit of visiting Friern Barnet Library, several times a week. In the early part of 2011, a small sign, headed 'strategic library review', appeared in the library but we didn't notice it until one of our children's friends pointed it out and told us what it meant: Barnet Council wanted to close our library.

As secretary of the school PTA I was well aware that 40 - 50% of local families speak English as a second language. Did Barnet Council think that these families would understand the phrase 'strategic library review' and complete a long consultation document? I spent time explaining to parents, children and teachers that our library was under threat of closure. Word was spreading from class to class, from school to school and the cry began to ring out: 'Save Friern Barnet Library!'

Public Consultation

Before making changes to any public services, Councils are legally obliged to conduct public consultation, to give due consideration to residents' views, to conduct Equality Impact Assessments and to provide mitigation for any adverse impact on the most vulnerable members of society.

'If the majority of the community values and wants to keep the library, this will surely come to light in the public consultation,' we thought. 'Barnet Council obviously doesn't realise how important FBL is to this community – we'll just have to show them!'

During the public consultation period, thousands of local people, from all walks of life, came together to create a powerful and passionate campaign to save the library. The Save Friern Barnet Library Group (SFBLG) emerged, a disparate group of people with a common determination to protect and preserve the library service and building for future generations.

Our children and their friends collected signatures for petitions, wrote to newspapers and MPs and took school assemblies; our three ward councillors all offered their support, we organised a Read-In at the library, a 'Walk to the Library Week' and several community parties on the village green. Home-made flyers appeared in windows and on lamp posts; over 3000 petition signatures were collected locally, and the huge wave of public support and awareness seemed likely to affect the outcome of the consultation. Indeed, the results of the consultation were to show that 91% of Friern Barnet residents wanted to keep their library.

I had never before been moved to campaign about anything and naively believed that our elected representatives would listen to the clear message from the community. It is strange now to remember a time when I trusted in the processes of democratic local government, when I believed that those individuals elected to represent us would all be honest and have the community's best interests at heart. Thus the first seeds of disillusionment were sown.

Foregone Conclusion

One of the first things the newly-formed Save Friern Barnet Library Group did was to request a meeting with Cllr. Robert Rams, the cabinet member responsible for the Barnet Strategic Library Review, and council officer Richard Grice. The meeting went ahead but we were asked not to record the meeting or to repeat any conversations that took place.

'Odd...,' we thought.

Early in the meeting, Hannah said that she was sad to think she wouldn't see 'her librarians' any more (I had seen in Council papers the plans to make many Barnet librarians redundant over the next two years).

Richard Grice looked my upset 10-year-old daughter in the eye and said, heartily, 'No librarian will lose their job,' adding in a scarcely-audible undertone, '...this year'.

It was sinister.

Local resident Alfred Rurangirwa then spoke about the huge importance of public libraries. A refugee from Rwanda, who had lost everything during the genocide, Alfred rediscovered in Friern Barnet Library a haven of books, community and education for his five children. We were bewildered by Robert Rams' response - he described volunteer libraries in Germany and ended by asking us if we would run a volunteer library in the middle of our local park.

'A challenge for you!' he said, grinning.

The Council's suggestion that we run a volunteer library in the middle of Friary Park was to reappear many times, despite our consistently negative response: the Save FBL Group did not support the idea of volunteer-run libraries replacing council-run, public libraries. Our campaign was to save Friern Barnet Library, a vital public service in a cherished public building!

The Save FBL Group looked at the Council's published proposals detailed in the Strategic Library Review. The word 'closure' did not appear anywhere in this document. Residents' views were instead sought on a so-called 'merger' between Friern Barnet Library and North Finchley Library. We were amazed to see that FBL had already disappeared from the map of Barnet libraries.

Councillor Robert Rams announced: 'Children are at the heart of this library review. Every primary school child will be taken into the library and become a member of the library.'

To us, this was a huge irony, because if Friern Barnet Library closed, regular class visits from nearby primary schools would no longer take place and hundreds and hundreds of children would no longer be able to walk to a local library after school. With jaw-dropping arrogance, Robert Rams suggested on his blog that local residents should each buy a Kindle.

At the Cabinet Meeting in July 2011, my daughter Hannah was the youngest person to ask a question:
'How does taking away our library 'increase reading, literacy and learning opportunities for children' in Friern Barnet? Why do the children of Friern Barnet not matter?'

Her question was brushed aside, along with many other serious questions from the community; the community's deep concerns about the impact this closure would have on residents were swept away as if mere inconveniences. The Cabinet voted for the closures, the phrase 'foregone conclusion' ringing out loud and clear.

Landmark Library - A Castle in the Air

After the cabinet meeting, Barnet Council announced that, following the closure of FBL, a 'Landmark Library' would be created in the artsdepot, a local theatre space. Our research showed that in 2002 Barnet Council had paid £100,000 to consultants to look into the possibility of the artsdepot housing a library but the space was declared unsuitable. No agreement was in place at artsdepot, no feasibility study had taken place, no lease had been agreed, no costings or detailed plans had been made, yet we were to believe that the Council would create this so-called 'Landmark Library'- trumpeted as 'one of the biggest and the best in London'- at artsdepot, somehow saving the Council money at the same time!

It was later revealed that Barnet Council had had no meetings with artsdepot whatsoever for the following eight months, whilst claiming that plans for a 'Landmark Library' at artsdepot were developing well. Many people feel that this grandiose project had only ever been a castle in the air, a smokescreen for library closures and the sale of public assets.

Newspeak – Ignorance is Strength

There followed a period of frustration, disbelief, anger and outrage. I had requested background papers from the Council, only to find that they were littered with serious misrepresentations of survey findings and financial inaccuracies. I was shocked to discover layer upon layer of exaggeration, careful manipulation of facts and figures and a blatant disregard for honesty.

Here are some examples:

- The findings of two very small focus groups were presented to Cabinet as if they represented the views of large numbers of the Barnet population, when sometimes the response quoted was that of only 4 people!

- Residents were invited to respond to council plans for 'fewer, bigger libraries', then the clearly negative response to this from the public was buried.

- Local schools were not contacted about the consultation until five school days before the end of the ten week consultation period (legally there should have been 'adequate time for the consultees   to   consider   the   proposals').

- Careful wording had been deliberately employed by Council officers in the preparation of consultation documents with the aim of obtaining nominal public support for broad Council strategy objectives, such as 'to increase reading, literacy and learning   opportunities   for   children'.

- Describing planned library closures as 'mergers' was part of a long-planned, Trojan horse strategy to disguise the sale of both Friern Barnet *and* North Finchley libraries.

Whilst it may be somehow legal to pretend to consult, only to ride roughshod over the community, it is not morally right. Public consultation is not legal if it is shown that the outcome was pre-determined, yet it became clear that the decision to sell FBL had been made long before the public was consulted. Immediately after the vote on the Library Strategy in July 2011, we were told by several members of Cabinet that our library needed to be sold and had been valued at £440,000. The costly, box-ticking exercise of public consultation had been a farce.

Members of the SFBL group undertook much research into the possibility of filing for Judicial Review. The group as a whole had serious doubts about the legality of the public consultation process.

The Community Library Process: Another Sham

At the end of July, Barnet Council announced the 'Community Library Process', saying that we had until 31 October 2011 to apply for an 'Expression of Interest' and 'submit proposals for a community use for the building'.

To quote Cllr Robert Rams in the local press: 'We have listened and offered those in Friern Barnet and Hampstead Garden Suburb [the chance] to come forward with a community use for the building or a facility in the area.'

We then had to prepare a detailed proposal by 8th January 2012. After working together through the busy Christmas holidays, the day came for the SFBL Group to hand over our proposal: a skeleton council-run library service at FBL supported by volunteers. Council officers then told us face to face that they would not consider our proposal for the building as the Council's intention had always been to sell the building for development. We had been misled into focusing our energy on a proposal that was destined to be rejected point blank.

Outraged, once again we turned our thoughts to filing for Judicial Review, only to find that the deadline for this legal process had just expired: Barnet Council had cleverly timed the Community Library Process precisely to this timetable.

Inevitably, the doors of our beloved library were closed on 5th April 2012. While many protested and joined a Sit-In, my focus was on consoling the children and taking flowers and a card to the devastated librarians. Our anger remained but we were utterly drained.

900 Mysteriously Disappearing Residents

A Scrutiny Committee Meeting had taken place in July 2011 at Hendon Town Hall, attended by many concerned residents. At this meeting everyone, including the Councillors, was most surprised to learn from Tom Pike (then Head of Libraries) that there would be 900 fewer people living in Coppetts Ward in the next five years. This extraordinary claim was at odds with the fact that at Holly Park School, a third Reception Class of 30 children had to be created the previous year as there were too few school places. I was most seriously concerned that all sorts of future provision for our area could be adversely affected by the Council's use of this strange data so I sent an enquiry to the Office of National Statistics. Here is an extract of the reply I received:

> 'In reference the map you highlighted from the (Barnet Council) report, ONS do not produce population projections at ward geographic level. The lowest ONS projections are calculated at local authority level. As such I do not know what source this would have been obtained from, or exactly how it was calculated.
> Quite what footnote 1 is trying to say I am not sure, but to my eyes it implies ONS produce ward-level projections, which we do not.'

The only data on Barnet population predictions produced by ONS clearly shows predicted population increase in every age group. It would appear that ONS predictions had been manipulated to show local population decline in an attempt to justify a reduction in our public services. Was this incompetence or deliberate deception?

Squatters and the People's Library

In September 2012, the unexpected arrival of the squatters, gave the whole community an enormous boost and really cheered us up. Seeing the library doors open once more was very moving for many local people.

Soon the squatters in conjunction with community volunteers were running a 'People's Library', donated books were being issued on an ad hoc basis with no date stamps or membership cards. However, our protest was being subverted and publicised as part of Cameron's Big Society in action: the way the People's Library was being perceived and reported in the press was dangerously close to playing into the hands of both Barnet Council and the Government. I felt very concerned that the anger that had sparked this 'People's Library' protest was being misread as enthusiasm for running a voluntary library ourselves.

I felt that if a library campaign group in the public eye went forward promoting volunteer-run libraries, it would harm the national campaign to fight for this country's public libraries. The fact is that, after an initial burst of enthusiasm, volunteer-run libraries often fail. For a working community like ours in Friern Barnet, I did not believe it could be sustainable – there is no local army of time-rich volunteers. And volunteers just can't do the job of trained, professional librarians. For me, the piles of random books on shelves and tables at the People's Library seemed more like a charity shop and could never compare to the deeply valuable service offered by public libraries.

I was afraid that this latest protest was backfiring. Had we scored an own goal?

After more than two years of fighting for our public services and welcoming Occupy squatters, it was with mixed emotions that I stood back while a group of residents negotiated with Barnet Council to establish a community-run Friern Barnet library. A hastily convened community trust was set up and took over the building 5th February 2012. Whilst they deserve every good wish for the success of this venture, this was not the ending I had fought for.

Disillusionment

The enlightened principle of free local access to books, funded and supported by Government to benefit all, is under threat: by 2016, it is predicted that 1000 local libraries may well have closed their doors. With Government hiding behind local authority cuts and abdicating responsibility, it is ordinary communities like ours who are desperately trying to rescue threatened libraries by running them ourselves. Yet, for me, each volunteer-run library represents another nail in the coffin of our invaluable public library service.

I have changed. My idealistic hopes and trust in local democracy are gone. I have witnessed cabinet members showing shocking contempt for members of the community. This has ranged from the tokenistic allowance for public questions at Hendon Town Hall - where genuine questions from residents are regularly given nonsensical or dismissive answers, in a parody of democracy - to hearing abuse of members of the public by persons such as Cllr. Brian Coleman which were met not with censure from other elected councillors but with laughter. I have been appalled to find that this disrespect for residents is ingrained in the processes of Barnet Council. For our children, lifelong library lovers who believed that their Council would listen to them, this has been an introduction to politics they will never forget.

BARNET ALLIANCE FOR PUBLIC SERVICES

BARBARA JACOBSON

Barnet Alliance for Public Services (BAPS) is a coalition of residents, workers and other campaign groups in the borough dedicated to maintaining and improving our public services. A public library is at the heart of a community, providing an array of services and benefits – access to printed reading material, films and CDs, the Internet, and information about local services and events as well as a place to study and for individuals and groups to meet. It's available to everyone, like a national health service for the mind and spirit. Residents endorse the importance of their local library through their usage, and they support it financially through their local taxes.

BAPS saw the potential loss of Friern Barnet Library not just as a blow to its immediate users and its staff but also to the wider community, as it would weaken the public library network in the borough. The promises made by Barnet Council about a replacement library were vague, unbudgeted, not certain and – most importantly – did not reflect what the residents wanted.

Furthermore, if this closure was not resisted, it would make all but the largest public libraries in the borough easy targets for the unthinking cost-cutters in the council. There was the fear that the sale of the building would be a negligible, short-term financial gain for the council – as had been the case with the closure and sale of Totteridge Library some years earlier – and a much bigger profit for a private developer. Naturally, BAPS actively supported the campaign to save Friern Barnet Library from the beginning of the threat to its existence.

The first steps in a campaign are always to raise awareness of the issues and gather support for the desired outcome. BAPS had been working on a number of campaigns at this time, including fighting the outsourcing of parking enforcement and the privatization of other public services under the 'One Barnet' banner, so we were able to help the Save Friern Barnet Library (SFBL) campaigners in planning and implementing strategies.

In our then still relatively brief experience we had learned that leaflets explaining the issues and putting forward the reasons for opposing or supporting an action are one of the most effective ways of reaching a wide audience. So BAPS contributed ideas and printed leaflets for SFBL and then we helped disseminate them, handing them out in the street and at the stalls we set up at different events around the borough. Similarly, we printed petitions against the closure and gathered signatures. BAPS helped draft press releases for SFBL, and its members were among those who wrote in protest to the local papers and to councillors. To be sure we reached as wide an audience as possible we always included information about the SFBL campaign in our newsletters and on our website.

We were sceptical about Barnet Council's offer to negotiate with the campaigners, as experience had led us to believe that such actions were mere window dressing. And so it proved. Thus, although Barnet Council's subsequent decision to close Friern Barnet Library angered members of BAPS, it did not completely surprise them. That the council would plough ahead with its plans regardless of what the local community adamantly made clear it wanted, was becoming par for the course. We greeted the news that this so-called negotiation was planned to last for three months apparently as a ploy to prevent the campaigners from bringing a judicial review within that critical deadline as an abuse of power and a cynical and morally corrupt action. Representatives of BAPS participated in the sit-in at the library on the day of the closure in April 2012 and displayed our banner in the windows.

The ideas of occupying the library and of organizing a pop-up library on the green space adjacent to Friern Barnet Library were discussed at BAPS' meetings. Although we did not occupy the building, we actively supported the members of the Occupy movement when they did, and we gave them our support during the court hearings. We participated in all the pop-up libraries, bringing donations of books and handing out more leaflets.

Sometime after the stock had been removed from Friern Barnet Library, BAPS went to the artsdepot, where the interim replacement library was said to be. There were no signs advertising or leading to it, but we found the single room into which a small proportion of the thousands of Friern Barnet books had been relocated. In a discussion with the librarian on duty we learned that this 'library' was open for a couple of hours a day, at different times of day on different days of the week. It was, therefore, not in the least surprising that attendance was only a few people a week.

When the library re-opened in its original location as the Friern Barnet Community Library, BAPS members responded wholeheartedly to the call to donate more books to stock the shelves and attended the first general meetings and various events.

BAPS continues to support the library, disseminating its newsletter to our mailing list and including information about its activities and its continuing campaign in our newsletters and on our website.

The Friern Barnet Community Library is a magnificent achievement, involving the community to an even greater extent than before and offering a wider range of activities. However, it is difficult to sustain a library forever on a voluntary basis, without a professional librarian and on a short lease. BAPS believes that the library should be a public service, funded and run by the council. A full-time professional librarian is needed to coordinate activities – even if some of these continue to be run by volunteers – organize systems, provide continuity and cohesion, and manage stock (an especially important part of keeping a library up to date and in line with the needs of its users). As a public library, Friern Barnet Community Library – and let it keep that name for ever – would gain strength from being within, and enhance, the wider library network. Residents have shown how efficiently and economically a library can be run, and the council should ensure it is run on public funds. Friern Barnet residents pay the same council taxes as residents elsewhere in the borough and are entitled to the same services. We look forward to the day when together we can bring this campaign to its full conclusion.

VILLAGE GREEN APPLICATION

HELENE ALDERMAN

Friern Barnet is rather short of recreational public space, and when in the course of the discussions about the future of the local library it was rumoured that there were plans to sell the building and the surrounding land for development, locals were concerned about the loss of a local recreational amenity as well as the potential loss of the library.

A suggestion was made in spring 2011 - in the course of discussions about the future of the library - that we might apply for village green status for the land surrounding the library. Initially many of us regarded the idea with some scepticism, but it was agreed that the possibility should be investigated.

The first thing was to investigate the requirements for registration as a village green. The relevant legislation is the Commons Act 2006. Section 15 (2) (a) which requires that 'a significant number of the inhabitants of any locality, or of any neighbourhood within a locality, have indulged as of right in lawful sports and pastimes on the land for a period of at least twenty years, and Section 15 (2) (b) they continue to do so at the time of the application'. (It does not have to be the same people over the twenty year period, and there is no definition of 'a significant number'.)

We were assisted by the Open Spaces Society's booklet on getting Greens registered. Crucially for us, the Friern Barnet and Whetstone Residents' Association joined the OSS thereby enabling us to get valuable guidance on procedure and the legal issues.

In parallel with our investigation into the procedural requirements, we had to collect evidence from people who had used the green area over the last twenty-three years for lawful sports and pastimes. Whilst this at first sight appeared a daunting task, through our contacts in the library group and the British Legion, we were able to build up a list of many who had used the green, and they in turn gave us further names.

We investigated extensively and inevitably found that some people were unable to complete these evidence forms for reasons of infirmity, disability or advanced age or simply because they did not feel capable of being called as witnesses at future Inquiry.

Nevertheless, between July and November 2011, 63 local, or former-local, users of the Green filled in the requisite form - based on an OSS recommendation - giving their accounts of how they had used or are continuing to use the Green.

Although there are areas of green space both to the east and the west of the library, we decided, to the disappointment of some, that there was insufficient evidence of use of the land to the east of the library to justify a claim to village green status.

Once we had the completed forms, we were required to acquire large scale OS maps and mark each individual's home on the map. (Processes such as these always accrue unanticipated expenses!)

The forms reflected the many and diverse activities which had been carried out on the green. In some cases people were able to remember back to the 1940's. Their anecdotes brought back further memories, so it became a journey into history. As well as individuals who had engaged in activities such as dog walking, meeting friends, building snowmen, bird watching, and team games, there were references to community events, including VE Day celebrations and other communal parties.

The application was put to the Council on 21 November 2011 in the names of the two local Residents' Associations, the Friern Village Residents' Association, and the Friern Barnet and Whetstone Residents' Association.

The Council responded formally in June 2012, stating that the land concerned was land acquired under the Public Health Acts 1875 et seq. and that it was already available to the public for recreational use.

The next step is for the Council to set up a public Inquiry, chaired by an independent inspector, who will adjudicate on the application. The inquiry is likely to be held towards the end of October 2013, which is after the time when this book goes to press.

A number of people, mainly from the Library group, put a lot of time,and in some cases, not insubstantial amounts of money, into this project. Although the idea arose in the context of the Library group, it rapidly developed a momentum of its own as it became apparent that the green was a valued resource in the community. This was evidenced by the fact that when the application was submitted to the Council, which as it was statutorily obliged to do, and objections were asked for, several hundred people wrote, apparently spontaneously, in support of the application. Apart from the Council itself, there were no other objections.

We hope that the application will succeed, but thanks to the library having a further lease of life, even if it is unsuccessful, the threat to the Green should be considerably lessened. Whether successful or not, as in the cases of the campaigns to save the library, and for the listing of the building, the Village Green project has been an impressive example of the community working together to preserve its assets.

Editor's Note: *Following an independent public inquiry, early 2014, an inspector recommended the council reject the application because it did not meet all the criteria under the Commons Act 2006. The Committee did just that and rejected the application for village green status in Friern Barnet.*

THE OCCUPY PHOENIX

ROSIE CANNING

On Tuesday 5th February, 2013 at midday, exactly five months since the occupation had begun on 5th September, 2012, and exactly ten months since the sit-in and closure on the 5th April, the Occupiers of Friern Barnet Library handed over the keys of the building to the local community. The local community - represented by eight trustees of the library - were on the verge of agreeing a two-year lease with Barnet Council (LBB) to run the library with a small amount of funding.

The community library received a licence from LBB to be in the library for two weeks with the promise of renewal of the licence if necessary to negotiate a lease and other matters (e.g. who pays the utilities, insurance, and ongoing future repairs). The council wanted to close the library for a few days, for what they called a 'deep clean', (rather a nasty term) and to then change locks and hand over the new keys to the trustees. The arrangement was met with animosity and suspicion. Eventually the council agreed to change locks and handover keys on the same day.

"This is a triumph for the local community," said Anne Storey, one of the trustees of the new community library. "Our library was closed in April. And we were told the building would be 'marketed'. Now we have our library back, with council financial support. We achieved this through constant campaigning, lobbying, and building a broad alliance including squatters, activists, supporters of the Occupy movement, local residents and library campaign groups."

Mr Greenacres, local activist said, "I do not fully understand this volte-face [by the council] but on the face of it, it's wonderful. However, we must not forget, this protest is not just about Friern Barnet Library, one library, it is also about the creeping move to a totalitarian state, the irrational, unjust and draconian cuts to vital public services and job losses that are undermining the very way we live, think and breathe. The anecdote is to wake up, open our minds, eyes and hearts and pledge continuing involvement and support to the Occupy Movement. Solidarity!"

Roger Tichborne, Local Blogger, Barnet Eye, said, "We should all remember that the council is *our* council. We are all part owners and stakeholders. What has happened in Friern Barnet is a massive victory because it has shown the whole community opposes these anti-social and unethical policies. It is up to each and every one of us to do everything in our power to resist the forces of ignorance and greed. We haven't got what we want, but we've got a community that stands together."

Housing and Squatting activist, Phoenix had the last word: "This campaign definitely shows the success of direct action and squatting. This is a seed of change. The whole country will soon be facing 80% of the rest of the cuts. They can take some inspiration from this direct action. We have collectively helped to save this library from being bulldozed and sold off for development. We would like to see more arrangements between owners of the 1.4 million empty buildings in the UK and squatter/ homeless and community groups, rather than the criminalisation being carried out by this government under the new law. A law we feel strongly is unjust, undemocratic and arbitrary. We want to make it clear that the activists support the National Libraries Campaign and that putting in place a paid librarian is a priority. I believe consensus has been reached with the community on this point. As it stands, the funding offered by the council does not cover a full time librarian, but as the two year lease is negotiated and plans go forward, this will be kept at the front of the conversation. The activists would like to say that we are strongly opposed to austerity and all the cuts, especially to the library service. We are also heavily opposed to criminalising the homeless/squatters. The extreme right of the conservative party is seeking to make squatting non-residential buildings also illegal. This, if it is successful, would affect all our rights to protest by occupying/squatting space, and would make successful community squat occupations such as the library campaign illegal, thus further removing our rights to shelter and protest."

As the library was being cleaned by the Occupy caretakers, ready for the handover of the keys and celebration, I was experiencing a mixture of feelings. Yes, I was pleased the building had been saved from demolition. It is a lovely single storey purpose-built library with original windows and features inside. On the one hand walking into the building and seeing the amazing selection of over 10,000 books, compared to the emptying shelves in the rest of the borough's libraries, is fantastic. But, now it was to be run as a community library, I was torn

146

between the victory and the loss of a public library. Any library that is run as a community venture is ultimately a loss of a public service.

I've got to know a lot of the community involved in saving the library and most of them are a lovely bunch of hard-working dedicated volunteers. My feelings were not about them. In my heart, my gut, I felt cheated. I knew that some councillors had been livid at the result of the court case. Not only was the validity of the protest upheld but, and this I suspect was worse, Barnet Council were directed to liase with the local community. They immediately set about putting some made-up rules in place. All of the community would have liked at least one of the occupiers to be a trustee, but the council refused to negotiate with any of them. And worse, the trustees were forbidden from calling the Occupiers, occupiers; they were to be called 'squatters'. This was only the first of many rules that divided the community and made the role of the trustees very difficult. There isn't room to discuss this further in this book.

Between the court case and the evening Bill Murphy appeared in the library with the statement, 'The council's position has shifted significantly...'

I wondered what change had taken place. I can only surmise, that although directed to liaise with Friern Barnet community, the council didn't really want to let go of the opportunity to sell the library and surrounding land to a developer. We must remember that this was always their goal. In some ways representatives of the council, and this is all they are, because they are not representing the citizens of the London Borough of Barnet, are like spoilt teenagers hell bent on getting their own way no matter what the cost.

We were soon to discover the real 'shift' in the council's rhetoric. There is a rather unsightly building opposite another library in Finchley Central. It is huge and worth millions. It has been sold to developers. Part of the deal includes a new 'landmark' (that awful word again) library. Cllr. Robert Rams was determined to have his 'landmark' library somewhere. According to plans it will be in the basement underneath the 74 exclusive Raison d'etre apartments. All this on the corner of what is already a very busy main road. Why not just keep the library in the ...library? So you see, another library is to be closed and the building and surrounding land sold. And of course clandestine meetings and secret lunches would have all been going on at the same time as the court case, maybe even before. It made the taste in my mouth putrid.

The Occupy Movement, Phoenix, Daniel, Donnie, Leon, Mark, and others brought with them an openess, acceptability and friendship of the like I had not experienced before. 'They were the best of times'.

147

When we sat around the table in the library sharing food and conversation, I seriously considered leaving my job and home to join them. I was in fact very sad they were leaving. Of course they were used to this, I thought. Finding a building to squat in or turn into a community project such as the Bank of Ideas in St Pauls and Occupy Justice in Hoxton. But when I went to the library after work and after the celebrations, I knew this was not the case.

For some of the occupiers, yes they had homes to go to or friends to stay with. But for some, they were moving on to another empty building, another squat, where in a matter of weeks or months they would go to court and be moved on once again. In amongst the hugs and good wishes, I could sense the sadness as we all knew things were changing.

The Occupy spirit that had arrived with Phoenix would be moving on too. There would now be a new community spirit that would have its own ideas of how a community library should run.

Occupy spirit was a strange phoenix-like beast that rose up and gathered the community into a better, more caring environment. Music, poetry, literature, art, conversation, protest, love, kindness, community, all this and more. And from this grew communication, ideas, cabaret, festivals, meetings and of course lots of tea and biscuits.

Stop Press: Rumour has it that five more libraries are under threat of closure in the land of Broken Barnet. And another so-called consultation is being hastily put together.
http://www.publiclibrariesnews.com/

THE CAMERA NEVER LIES

LUCY NOWELL

Friern Barnet Library is the closest library to where I work. I used to pop in at lunchtimes or after work, mainly to use the internet and sometimes to browse through the books. I visited a couple of libraries elsewhere in Barnet, but was shocked to learn the most convenient for me was to close.

I was at work on April 5th 2012 when in the afternoon I heard there was an occupation at the library. I was on a late shift and frustratingly couldn't get there until 5.30pm; but luckily I had a small video camera with me. There was a large crowd of people gathered outside, including Mr Greenacres, with his bike and trailer covered in 'We love our library' posters, keeping everyone entertained using a public address system run on a portable amp, and informing us a portion of chips was making the rounds - a welcome relief for those who had waited outside all afternoon and were beginning to feel cold.

About 5:50pm, the library doors started to move. I had my camera ready to film the Friern Barnet Library's first occupiers who emerged, amongst them Maureen Ivens, Fiona Brickwood, Tirza Waisel and Famous Five Barnet Blogger Vicki Morris. Some, like Keith Martin, punched the air with their fists to the thunderous cheer of the crowd. Maureen Ivens, from Save the Friern Barnet Library campaign, was the first to give a speech thanking everyone for their support and food whilst occupying the building; and to continue the struggle to reopen the library.

Speeches also mentioned how local people had been tricked, taken for a ride and treated with contempt by the council. There was also anger at the library being closed early on the final day. I didn't edit the film until four months later, and uploaded it on YouTube on 10th August 2012. I made the video just short of five minutes, and finished it with the words: 'The End ...or is it?' little realising that in less than a month, it would actually be re-occupied.

After the first occupation, local businessman and 'Barnet Eye's' blogger, Roger Tichborne, made a brilliant suggestion of having a 'pop-up' library on the green outside Friern Barnet library on 14th April 2013. I filmed this and subsequent pop-up libraries that were held every weekend. These events were well supported by the local community, including the Famous Five Barnet Blogger Mr Mustard (who brought a case of 'banned' books), Mrs Angry (whose clear and humorous analysis of council meetings in her 'Broken Barnet' blogs made me actually understand what was going on, and prompted me to film them later), Mr Reasonable, and Roger Tichborne himself.

Stalls were also erected on the library green by groups such as the Green Party, Barnet Alliance for Public Services (BAPS) and UNISON which, through Barnet Trades Council, supported the campaign to save Friern Barnet Library. At the time of the first pop-up library, a cherry tree at the bottom of the library's green had come into blossom, and looked beautifully serene. I felt an affinity with this tree, and took several still photographs; its' canopy provided natural shelter from heavy rain at a later 'Pro-democracy' pop-up library.

Standing underneath this tree at the end of the first pop-up library day, Roger said: "The more often we have this, the more often people come, the more likely we're gonna have the library re-opened."

His sentiments echoed the determination, defiance and resilience of the community.

The pop-up library was taken on tour later in the year. A gazebo was placed outside Osidge and East Barnet libraries, the latter where Councillor Robert Rams, cabinet member for libraries and architect of the Strategic Libraries Review (that included plans for a 'landmark' library merging Friern Barnet and North Finchley libraries), held his surgeries. Unfortunately, Robert Rams was not there on the day, but another cabinet member, Councillor Joanna Tambourides appeared, and truculently answered our probing questions regarding library closures and the One Barnet Programme, particularly on mass outsourcing council services. After she left, there was a ceremonial book–burning (no books were actually harmed).

In June 2012, I was offered a place to stay nearer to work, which I gratefully accepted. The 60 mile drive to my home was proving more stressful with the increase of filming activities in Barnet at the weekends. The first evening before arriving at my new abode, I tried to film a council meeting at the Town Hall in Hendon, from the middle of three rows of seating allocated for the public gallery. Before proceedings began, the Head of Governance approached me and asked who I was and what I was doing, before conveying a message from the chairman of the meeting, Councillor Brian Coleman, saying the camera was 'obtrusive' and to stop filming.

As far as I was aware, the Council had agreed to allow filming the year before. However, I took my camera off the tripod and listened to the rest of the meeting. This was not the last time this chairman was to show disapproval of being filmed; and I was fortunate not to suffer physical harm from his wrath. The story was reported in the local online paper the next day, with statements from Mrs Angry and Barnet Council's opposition Labour leader, Councillor Alison Moore, condemning the chairman's decision. Later the same day, in the evening, I filmed another council meeting, chaired this time by Barnet Council's Leader, Councillor Richard Cornelius, and was joined by three other residents filming from the front row of the public gallery. We were allowed to film the meeting unopposed. In my view, filming council meetings actually helps local democracy, in making local government more transparent.

On 31st July 2012, I filmed Rosie Canning giving a speech to the Scrutiny and Overview Committee at Hendon Town Hall about Friern Barnet Library, due to the fact that a petition of over 2,500 signatories had been amassed to re-open it. Rosie spoke about the damaging effects the library closure had on the local economy and outlined alternatives. Local ward councillors Labour's Pauline Coakley-Webb and Barry Rawlings, and Conservative's Kate Salinger all passionately put their points across to make a last minute heart-felt plea to the Council, to recommend a change to re-open this well-loved library; ultimately to no avail, despite the local cross-party consensus, proving local people have no influence on policy. This was heard by at least 50 supporters in the public gallery. Tensions rose when Barnet Council's Assistant Director for Customer Services including libraries at the time, Bill Murphy, began to speak. Mr Greenacres called out in disagreement. The ruckus that followed led to a security guard being called, and the committee chairman, Hugh Rayner, deciding on a 15 minute recess of the meeting for things to calm down.

On Barnet council's proposed merger of Friern Barnet with North Finchley libraries, Councillor Kate Salinger said: 'I imagined the artsdepot landmark library would rise phoenix-like out of the ashes, to show the rest of the borough what a proper library would look like'. In reality, after visiting it, she found it to be 'a paltry sop to the people of Friern Barnet.' As we all know, the phoenix that did help save Friern Barnet library five weeks later was Phoenix Rainbow himself.

In September 2012, after 'occupying' a camp bed in an attic study for three months, I got used to having just a few and essential personal possessions around me, including my computer and camera. The

151

arrival of the occupiers at Friern Barnet Library seemed for me very timely. I empathised with their transient, nomadic lifestyle, focusing on what's really important; one's friends and the community. A very aptly named Phoenix Rainbow was the spokesperson of the band of people occupying the library - breathing new life into the wonderful old building.

The first meeting between people from the Occupy Movement, Save Friern Barnet Library Group and officers from Barnet Council was held on the first Monday morning after the 5th September 2012 occupation; but the officers did not want it filmed. However, there were bloggers there and they reported the meeting so accurately that future meetings had to be as genuine and open as possible. This helped ensure there was no ambiguity between the council, occupiers and the community.

News soon spread about the occupation; this was a community fighting back, for library closures were happening all over the country as councils failed to grasp their importance. Phoenix is a charismatic man and has over twenty years expertise in homelessness and squatting rights. News media warmed to him, with international film crews as well as national newspapers wanting to hear the library story. Throughout all this, I filmed whenever I could. I filmed library events and visits from external media, keeping my own locally filmed timeline of the exciting events as they evolved, and acquiring extensive and unique film footage in the history of the 'occupied' library. This later attracted the interest of film-makers Oonagh Cousins (A Polite Revolution) and from France, Irene Sinou, who delighted in my treasure trove of rich source material.

The weekly 'Open Mic' sessions, Cabaret and Earth Circus events were a real treat, bringing artists and musicians together from across the world. It was during this time my confidence grew in my colleague Donald Lyven, who helped me with filming, and whose distinctive plummy voice is not too unlike his namesake Donald Sinden. My favourites of the Occupied Library events were the spoken word poetry from, most memorably, Anna Chen (reading her Anna May Wong poem), the energetic Pete the Temp and Edinburgh Fringe Slam Poetry Winner, Cat Brogan. At the end of the five hour spectacular Cabaret in December 2012, Phoenix, who had been comp→èring the show, gave a rousing and emotive speech, which to this day, I regret I could not film. I was unprepared for this finale, and had exhausted my supply of digital video films and still camera's space on an SD card; a warning that in future, I must keep something in reserve for the unexpected.

It's unfortunate in England that courts do not allow proceedings to be filmed, although tweeting is sometimes allowed. Local blogger Mrs Angry tweeted and later blogged a detailed report of the first eviction court case against the Occupiers, for which I was grateful as I was unable to attend in person. Barnet Council's legal department had underestimated local feelings and the strength of argument the Occupiers put forward which resulted in an adjournment and a new date set for a full Court hearing. In addition to this, Barnet's legal team mislaid a briefcase of documents immediately after the court proceedings, much to the glee of the gathered supporters. There was a bit of a celebration that evening, and the hearing gave much needed publicity to the fight.

On 17th December 2012 the second court hearing took place. I was unable to attend on the first day, but I was amused at the names of the barristers: for Barnet Council, Nicholas Grundy; and for the Occupiers, Sarah Sackman who did the library proud. They sounded like characters from a Dickens novel. Fiona Brickwood, Phoenix and Keith Martin gave excellent evidence in support of the library, and Barnet Council gave their side. During the lunch recess, just before the afternoon's court proceedings began, I overheard Nicolas Grundy talk about his itchy wig, and how it was made from horse hair. I wondered mischievously, which end of the horse it came from.

I really wished I could have filmed the next day when Judge Patricia Pearl (who had an amiable twinkle in her eye like Ann Robinson) delivered her judgement. It was like one of those television court room dramas. Emotions were being tugged in one direction and then another as she spoke. She mentioned all the aspects of the case and we were not sure until the final sentences which way it was going to go. Her recommendation was that the Council had to discuss the option of giving a licence to the Occupiers to run the library; they were allowed until the end of January 2013 to come up with a solution. This deadline focused the minds of both sides, and meant the eviction would not take place before the festive season was over.

When the day-time library meetings were moved to the evenings, and without council officers present, more people including myself were able to attend, and eventually the meetings were always filmed. I thought people would play up to the camera; but disagreements and conversation flowed as naturally as before, dispelling my concerns. Much of the filming was never made public due to the sensitive nature of the talks at the time and not wishing to jeopardise the volunteers' position with the council. One exception to this was when Assistant Director, Bill Murphy, attended on 10th January 2013, hoping to repair damage done by remarks Councillor Rams had made on the library occupation a week earlier. Bill Murphy also announced 'the council's position has changed' and 'shifted significantly' on the future of Friern Barnet library. What he'd said was uploaded to YouTube for everyone to see what the council were prepared to do. This was a dramatic breakthrough as he didn't mind being filmed revealing the council's new stance.

When the library was handed over to the trustees on the 5th February, 2013, Sarah Sackman wisely said, "What binds us together, this care for the community, is so much stronger than the market-value of a building". How true her words were. Phoenix made everyone hold hands and dance around the cherry tree on the library's green, singing: 'Stand up, Stand up, Stand up for the library.'

I filmed them all, dancing around *my* tree – it just seemed to be so fitting; everything had come full circle.

A PERSONAL JOURNEY

FIONA BRICKWOOD

During the library sit-in, the council, feeling in need of reinforcements, called the police. We heard that the police weren't unduly interested in our well-mannered little protest but they did pop in, took one look at our group, muttered "Middle Aged, Middle Class" and departed.

Casting an eye over our motley group, I wondered whether this assessment was accurate. Were we just a mild mannered Grey Brigade? Throughout our campaigning, what I had seen in their faces was intensity and concentration as, week by week, we developed the campaign, researching; analysing council reports; challenging council meetings; figuring out our strategies for protests; press releases. I had barely noticed the lines of life experience etched on some of our faces.

I daresay that I fitted the policeman's mental image. It was my first experience of civil disobedience, after half a century of being a law abiding citizen. The past year had seen my first experiences of taking part in protests and asking questions in council chambers. The months that followed our sit-in would see my first time of taking part in a court case (as a defence witness). Many of us were protest virgins, entering the fray quite late in life.

Now that I am more keenly aware of the importance of taking part in protests, I feel some remorse that I had not started this important work earlier.

Yet entering the fray brings its own benefits to those who take part. Working within the protest group brings a continual stream of challenges. There is much to learn, many difficult strategies to work out. Passions are rampant; disagreements within the group abound and are hard fought. Fellow campaigners become close comrades – and also people whom you often have an urge to beat about the head with a rolled up copy of the Barnet Times!

This long battle has been relentlessly demanding, and the fruits of this labour are commensurately rich, in the knowledge, life experience, friendship and personal growth it provides. I have seen this in my fellow campaigners as well as in myself.

It has brought me to some watershed moments. My first was being interviewed for Radio 4's PM programme. Only a momentary broadcast, yet those who know how painfully shy I was in my youth, know how significant it was for me to find myself able to speak to millions of Radio 4 listeners.

As a child, I was too afraid to speak out in class; horrified whenever the teacher called on me to say something in front of my 30 classmates. Treacherous blushes that exposed my embarrassment only added to my mortification. School was a pretty wretched experience.

It has taken half a century to overcome this shyness. Speaking live on Radio 4 to millions of listeners was a watershed moment. I felt that, finally, I had cast off the psychological braces of my childhood.

Standing in the witness box was a second watershed moment. With so much resting on our court case, and with our campaigners watching intently, the pressure was on. In my youth, I could never have imagined putting myself in this position but, after fifty years of building resilience, I felt no fear. As I looked down from the witness pulpit onto the prosecution barrister, I felt like Miss Jean Brodie scowling at the headmistress. I felt strong. As I felt stronger, I felt his arrogance weaken; felt his potency go flaccid. This time, the blushes were not mine.

This was a journey over fifty years, but it had accelerated powerfully over these past two years of campaigning. Not only for me: others in our group have also gained in strength and confidence. Something about this passionate campaign had led to achievements internally as well as externally.

But what had induced ordinary residents to throw ourselves into this demanding battle and fight with such determination? It was rather more than just protesting the loss of our local library. Certainly we were all very passionate about that, with varying emphases on the importance of protecting the local library facility and that of saving this beautiful, historic building from those councillors who could appreciate neither its beauty nor its history.

Most importantly (in my view), losing our library would have meant losing our community. It is the only public building in Friern Barnet; the only place where local people can meet, network, and discuss what matters to us. It is, in effect, our village hall. When the council had been running it as a library, they had not understood its importance as a community hub and had not facilitated this usage, but once we, the people, took it over, it once more became the heart of our local community.

Our passion for these protests had been fuelled by our outrage at the council trying to sell what was *ours*. It was not theirs to sell. If thieves enter your home to sell off your possessions, the police will answer your distress call and take these criminals away in handcuffs. Yet, when the council tries to flog off our libraries – and with that, our heritage - the police can do nothing. The law stands idly by while these councillors in their striped jerseys make off with our valuables in broad daylight.

Is "theft" too strong a term for this invidious act? The legal definition of theft is taking something without the owner's consent and with intent to permanently deprive the owner thereof.

On the question of ownership, the library belongs to us, the people. The council owns *nothing*. Everything that any council or government "owns" is merely held in trust for the people. *We*, not they, are the true owners.

On the issue of consent, the fact that this sale of *our* library was being progressed against our wishes is evidenced by the council's own consultation. In 2011, the council did a major "Library Strategy Consultation". They asked whether we agreed with their proposal to [dispose of] Friern Barnet and North Finchley libraries to build their so-called "Landmark" library. The answer was an unequivocal "No!" 91% of respondents from Friern Barnet, and 73% of respondents across the whole borough, stated that they disagreed with this proposal.

The council ignored the result of their consultation, our petitions and protestations. They just went ahead with what *they* wanted to do, showing that the consultation was a sham. We were incensed.

Surely selling our possessions without our consent and against our express wishes is misappropriation? I don't understand why the law gives us so little protection against such acts committed by our council.

No doubt the council believed that their "Landmark" library would be an improvement as it would be much bigger and have more facilities. They could not comprehend that people want a *local* facility that children and old folk can walk to, run into friends, and be known by the staff.

They seemed not to care that Friern Barnet Library is a part of our local heritage. Selling it would have destroyed what their forebears gave us, financed in part by the generosity of the Carnegie Trust in 1934, discarding the altruism of their gift.

They did not consider how losing our only community space would damage the social cohesion of our community. Nor did they realise how damaging this loss would be to the local economy. Many of the little shops in Friern Barnet struggle to survive because, although we are on a busy road, motorists cannot easily park to pop in. After the council closed the library in April 2012, local shops reported a drop in takings. They had lost the casual purchases of library visitors. After the library was re-opened by Occupy in Sept 2012, the footfall increased, as did their sales.

We did not believe the council's insistence that they "needed" the £430,000 from its sale. This paltry sum would have dropped into the bowels of the council funds, disappearing instantly without trace. A pittance.

So how can councils be permitted to plunder our assets, acting in direct contradiction to the results of their own consultations? Councils across Britain are doing this; flogging off the assets they hold in trust for their residents, against the wishes of those residents. How is it that councils are allowed to get away with this behaviour?

Unfortunately, each time a council plunders the assets it holds in trust for its residents, it validates similar actions by other councils. Each council justifies these actions by pointing at its neighbour: "Well they did it, so it must be alright".

Each time residents fight back, it helps to counter this justification. But these fights need to be effective. Giving an errant council a bloody nose may release some frustration, but it's not enough. Our protests and petitions were not enough: we needed the direct action of Occupy, and the legal challenges of Leigh Day.

Residents of Friern Barnet are enormously grateful to Occupy and to Leigh Day, for it was only through Occupy's direct action, and Leigh Day's altruistic support, that we have been able to reclaim our library, our community, and our rightful inheritance. Communities across the country have reason to be grateful for the actions which may help to prevent their councils from following suit.

The battle for Friern Barnet library was not happening in isolation. It was one of several battles that have been going on in Barnet within the last five years or so. This wave of protests against the council has been dubbed "The Barnet Spring".

One such battle is the campaign by the high street traders of North Finchley. They protested that the council's huge hikes in parking charges were hurting them badly. Some had gone out of business as the high cost of parking was driving people to shop elsewhere.

With their protests similarly dismissed by the council, the traders banded together and launched a campaign to ask people to vote out the Cabinet member responsible for these excessive parking charges. The public responded, voting Brian Coleman off the London Assembly in May 2012. Recognising the strength of this uprising, the Leader of Barnet Council removed Coleman from his Cabinet position and brought in someone else to address the parking problems.

The Battle of Friern Barnet Library and the Battle of the North Finchley Traders have been won. Tragically, the Battle of "One Barnet" was lost, and this may cost Barnet dearly. "One Barnet" is the council outsourcing an unprecedented amount of council services to the profit-making giant Capita, who have promised to do them for far less money.

Quite how Capita will achieve this is not well understood, especially as they will *increase* our costs by taking their profits out of our pot, plus corporation tax and business rates. Councils don't pay any of these when they provide the services themselves. Many of us think the council has naively bought the salesman's magic beans.

Everyone – including the council – is extremely worried about what happens if "One Barnet" fails. Statistically, a quarter of all outsourcing projects fail. If 'One Barnet' fails, our council leader acknowledges that it will be a total disaster for Barnet. As Barnet is handing over £1 billion of our money to Capita for this ten year contract, it has been dubbed the "Billion Pound Gamble".

Residents and workers have been pleading with the council to consult with us to work out better alternatives, but they refused. In the judicial review, the judge said Barnet had acted illegally by failing to consult but, after protracted legal arguments, he ruled that that the JR was out of time.

All these battles have this common denominator of a council unwilling to sit down with residents and staff, to work out a solution that works. All these campaign groups are driven by highly intelligent, extremely knowledgeable people. Many council staff are also highly intelligent, knowledgeable. Each has different sets of knowledge and different ways of thinking. Pooling these different sets of knowledge, ways of thinking, philosophies, and ideas can produce something far better than anyone can produce separately.

It is puzzling that the council is so loathe to have meaningful consultations. Perhaps this is because it is outside their experience and culture to do so. The council is used to working within its own offices, keeping its discussions within a protective perimeter. There is little intercourse of thinking and knowledge between council and the residents. It is then very hard to pull down these walls and engage in constructive dialogue.

For the library, we *did* have this constructive dialogue, and it started in the most unlikely way: between Occupy squatters and senior council officers. Even more bizarrely, these meetings were initiated and facilitated by Phoenix, the principal squatter! The council officers found the experience richly productive; not something to be feared, after all. This earlier experience may well have made it easier for the council to follow the judge's advice to work co-operatively with us to develop plans to run the community library. I think the council would agree that, in these tentative steps towards working co-operatively, both parties have benefitted from each other's knowledge and experience.

A PLACE OF REFUGE

AN INTERVIEW WITH ALFRED RURANGIRWA

How did you get involved with the Library?

We were new in the Friern Barnet neighbourhood in December 2008 and I was out walking with my children; the youngest of whom was five years old and the oldest was eighteen. During our walk one of them pointed at a building with excitement, saying: "Look, there's a library here."

My first impression was, "A very beautiful building!"

We went inside and were warmly welcomed by the librarian ladies, who showed us around. We joined straight away. That was my first contact!

Something in particular touched me when I was looking at the books; I found classical books on Greek history and mythology and Ancient Rome. That was amazing!

In Rwanda, I had been studying Greek, Latin and modern languages and had gained an interest in the classics. During the genocide in Rwanda, all my student notes and books had been burned, simultaneously with my family home. At that painful time (1994), my family was wiped out.

How did you get involved with the Save Friern Barnet Library Action group?

I was in the library when Maureen and Kim were saying they'd heard a rumour about it being closed. I was absolutely horrified because the library meant a lot to me and my children. The children were continually borrowing books to research their homework and they also used the library's computers to print homework out. They met other children there and started to make friends. For me, as a lone parent, it was a safe place where I could leave my children and go shopping and also do some work. As soon as the news about closure was confirmed, I started to put the first petition online, which required 3,000 signatures! Of course Maureen and Kim advised me, but the petition was in my name. My children were of course devastated and helped in distributing flyers. It was very helpful to have 5 children who were so committed to saving the library. They went to the Town Hall twice and even asked questions there.

How did you hear about the squatters?

Come on, Rosie; first allow me to talk about your Re-open Friern Barnet petition which in fact revived our morale. It made a really good impact as you defended it very well in the live debate at the Council Chambers with one-to-one arguments and counter-arguments! It was a hot meeting that will not be forgotten. From that night onwards, I hoped that we would see our library reopened one day. And from then onwards, our Save Friern Barnet group redoubled its efforts to collect signatures for the Reopen Friern Barnet petition. We targeted all areas and I remember having been the first to approach my local post office. I explained to the manager, who used to chat with me, that we needed at least 7,000 signatures for the second petition. He immediately allowed me to leave a couple of petitions with pen attached at the post office so that the customers while queuing could see them and sign. More than that, he offered for himself and his colleagues to keep an eye on them and guard those which were fully signed, advising me to pass by frequently, not only to collect them but also to bring others and so on...

I am telling you, we got thousands of signatures in that post office. I was so excited by this outcome that I decided to approach the Cooperative supermarket. We collected a good number of signatures from them too. On my way back home, I also put the Re-opening petitions in Friern Barnet dental clinic, at Friern Barnet Town Hall, Krishna Vision on Friern Barnet Road and Holly Park Clinic. All of them kindly accepted, as they had provided the same service for the first petition.

One lady in Holly Park Clinic asked, "Do you think this time the Council will reopen the library?"

I said, "Let's not give them a reason not to... we must simply obtain enough signatures."

She smiled and wished me good luck. There was a lot of goodwill in the community towards our efforts. And believe me, we were about to reach 7,000 signatures when I heard that some "awe-inspiring guys had 'parachuted' out of thin air into the library".

I think it was during one of the Save Friern Barnet Library group meetings.

I asked myself, "Are we in the middle of one of the ancient Greek myths?"

I had heard that one of the guys was called Phoenix and that their group was well organised and prepared to occupy the library until Barnet Council and the residents could reach an agreement to reopen it.

I said to myself, "Is this a repeat of the Trojan wars? Am I going to see the Trojan War played out live? Phoenix - will he be the angry Achilles, the greatest of the Greek heroes or Agamemnon, the Commander in chief? And who will be Hector, the Trojan hero?"

Also I heard there was a lady among the group called Thalia (one of the nine muses). Would she continue to delight her fellow occupants in a sweet and harmonious voice?

Then the idea came to me that the sit-in was perhaps the Trojan Horse!!!

What did you think?

The fact that the library was reopened because of the squatters seemed to me to be our last chance and it was crucial for the Save Friern Barnet Library group to mobilise the community in order to prevent the library doors closing again. I think that I was the only one in the SFBL meeting who said we should support the squatters that first night when Phoenix arrived. I was so eager that all the residents should stand behind them and give them full support. I think the others were too scared.

What was it like when the doors were opened again?

As I said at the beginning, it was as if a miracle had become a reality: It was unbelievable. I was so delighted that I hugged everybody in sight.

What did it mean to you to use the library again?

It meant for me that we can be effective if we stand together. When people work together, they have a chance to succeed. It meant to me that having different views in a group is not a big problem if everyone remains positive and honest. Mutual respect is essential.

Lend me your ears, Mrs Rosie. It is imperative that we keep the building beautiful, especially by ensuring the outside of it (the front of it, its sides and the green space) are kept clear and tidy, as first impressions are always the most important !

And we want to offer adults and children a welcoming and pleasant environment.

How did you feel?

I was excited to see so many people were mobilised and united to save the library which had refused to die.

How did you feel at the end of the two days?

I was happy because at the end of the day the decision of the judge did not confirm the closure of the library.

What do you hope for the library in the future?

I hope it will continue to be an illustration of harmony between people.

I hope it will continue to be a symbol of dialogue where selfishness, intrigues and treachery have no place.

I hope it will continue to reflect courage, ability, strength, and excellence.

I hope it will continue to inspire the young generation that good behaviour, honesty and perseverance can make the impossible possible.

I hope it will continue to help in the improvement of reading and education in general.

I hope it will continue to be a place for music, poetry, dancing, games, food and drink, meetings and discussions; a centre for feasting and fun, a place which gives an opportunity to entertain friends and revitalise and value cultures.

SQUATNEY WICK

DONALD LYVEN

In late January 2013, I received an invitation to attend the premiere of 'A Polite Revolution', an independent film made by Oonagh Cousins. Oonagh is a filmaker, photographer and writer, who makes work that contributes towards positive social change. She had been in Friern Barnet for the previous few weeks, filming the Occupy Movement's involvement in the Library saga, highlighting the excellent work they were doing in raising the issues of homelessness and inequality in our skewed society.

On the appointed day Lucy Nowell and I started to plan our journey, but there was one minor problem: we only had a sketchy text message about making our way to Hackney Wick railway station. Once there, we did not know exactly where to go. We were to look for posted messages. I elected to drive - despite the car's reluctance to start without a push - as it seemed the quicker option, not being acquainted with East London overground rail services; or with East London! Shortly after 7pm, Lucy and I set off; diligently following the sat nav's instructions on how to reach Hackney.

The streets around the station were deserted, and parking was not a problem. It was a cold clear night, too cold for standing idly about, so at the forecourt we rang a mobile number and were given our instructions. We were to follow a steep muddy path, where we hung on to iron railings to assist our progress and eventually we arrived at a deserted 1960s industrial park and a dark abandoned warehouse; the sort of place where Scooby-Doo and the team might start one of their adventures!

After waiting a short time, an Occupier with a bike joined us and suddenly a door opened... There was light! We entered the warm building and were welcomed with hugs and kisses, to what the Occupiers had nick-named 'Squatney Wick'. We were then given a quick tour of the property where the offices either side of a long corridor had been turned into bedrooms or private study spaces.

Everything was organised and even the bathrooms were in full working order.

We then entered a large chamber which had numerous 'reclaimed' armchairs and settees. Suspended from the ceiling was a massive army camouflage net complete with synthetic leaves. At the rear was a large storage, kitchen and serving area where a delightful buffet was gradually appearing, and a big steaming cooking pot was simmering away full of an aromatic vegetable curry.

It was explained that the Occupiers were there in full knowledge of the landlord, who thought it more sense having people living there than paying for security to keep out potential vandals, arsonists, and drug takers. More people arrived, including Occupiers we recognised from Friern Barnet, as well as familiar local people associated with the library. The atmosphere was exceptionally friendly and all-embracing as we put our money in the donations box and ate our plates of curry and rice and other refreshments.

With the Community Library soon to start a new chapter, there was much to reflect upon: the duplicitous action of council officers who had started legal proceedings when still in negotiations with the Occupiers; the deliberate damage to the roof allowing rainwater to ingress the fabric of the building; the ridiculous expense of opening the 'pocket' library at the artsdepot, and the actions of Councillor Robert Rams – the cabinet member responsible for the whole costly mess. Now he was making a fuss because he was sent a few texts and a joke greetings card at Christmas from the library.

Could I ever trust my council again on anything? Probably not. Getting involved in the library campaign led to me joining Barnet Alliance for Public Services (BAPS) and becoming politically active again. Attending council meetings was a real eye opener; the antics of renegade council members such as Cllr. Brian Coleman have to be seen to be believed. Reading the articles from the famous five Barnet Bloggers was very enjoyable; especially Mrs Angry, whose inventive and humorous writings can explain the complexities of council process – or more likely, abuse of – better than anyone.

I'm not one of the heroes in the library story. I didn't do that much and in the process I had a great time. I sat in at meetings, took photos at the numerous and varied library events, including live music evenings, the Will Self book launch, the Halloween party, and the many Earth Circus Concerts of music, crazy stories and poetry. Throughout all this, I ate a lot of cake! I also assisted in constructing the defences of the library in case the court case had gone against the Occupiers, to prevent bailiffs entering the building; it's amazing what you can find in skips. Oh, and I designed the Library's Winter Seasons' greeting card that was sent to many influential local people.... and more importantly, this was the place I met Lucy for the first time.

At Squatney Wick, we numbered nearly a hundred people by the time proceedings started, and so we sat down and listened to various impromptu speeches, notably from Leon, Oonagh and Keith Martin. Eventually the lights were dimmed. People hushed, the makeshift white sheet screen hanging from the ceiling quivered and the film started.

I implore anyone who hasn't seen this film to seek it out. As a piece of modern social history it is fascinating to see how society is still so divided. Social justice still has a long way to go, and is not helped currently by the most divisive government ever to rule this country. Various cheers went up whenever someone from the library featured or a snippet of Lucy's filming appeared. But the narrative did have an enduring message; great things can be achieved when people stand together and not blindly accept whatever mad-cap decisions our daft rulers dictate.

Applause and a big cheer greeted the end of the film and the evening evolved into one tremendous party, especially on hearing that the film had achieved over four thousand views on the Internet! New people were still arriving and the place was heaving as the sound system belted out music.

It was approaching midnight when I gathered a group together to return to the Borough of Barnet. We said our goodbyes to the Occupiers and thanked them for their wonderful hospitality. It was decided though to leave by a different route, and so we were led to an adjoining room, containing many bicycles - the transport of choice for any free-spirited caring soul - and departed through a rear exit. It was a longer walk back to Hackney Wick Station but not so treacherous underfoot.

The car started first time despite the cold, and the sat nav - as always - miraculously led us back to Barnet. The talk on the journey home was of success, but the struggle to get Friern Barnet Library reopened was, of course, just one important battle with the council. The relentless conflict the current administration seem to be waging against its citizens concerning high street parking, cuts in services and mass privatisation continues; and hopefully will all be told one day in a film called: The Battle of Barnet II.

Editor's footnote: By the time of going to press, former Barnet Mayor, Cllr. Brian Coleman had been expelled from the Conservative Party for attacking Helen Michaels, proprietor of Café Buzz in North Finchley, and further disgraced by being found guilty of calling a Friern Barnet resident a "t***" at a council meeting in April 2012, when he asked a question at a cabinet meeting. However, the former Cllr was found not guilty by the Group Leaders' Panel of failing to treat others with respect when he referred to the public gallery at a September 2012 full council meeting as the "sad, mad and a couple of hags". (Source: Times series, Thursday August 6th 2013).

THE END OF THE OCCUPATION

PETE PHOENIX

In twenty-five years of setting up community projects in empty and unused buildings, we had never seen such a phenomenal level of local community support. When we entered the library it was completely bare, with three walls of empty bookshelves. Within eight weeks we had 8,000 books filling the shelves. As someone said, 'every book was a vote to keep the library open'. And by the time of the key handover, some five months later, there was somewhere in the region of 12-14,000 books. At the beginning of the occupation, we asked everyone for two things: to volunteer and to bring us books. It gave our hearts great joy as young and old trooped through the doors with carrier bags, boxes and car boots full of books.

We slept in the library on a rota basis with a core crew of eight to ten people, although in fact about four people lived there for the duration of the occupation. One thing we want to make clear is that we were campaigning for a public library service with paid librarians rather than a volunteer-only service. We ran a basic interim library service run on a trust basis. This basic system was set up by some of our five friendly qualified librarians. There was some talk in the media about the 'Big Society', which is a code word for shutting down our hard won public services and selling them off to private companies that are linked to government ministers and government sponsors. We ran a voluntary system in our squatted community centres out of love for community. Not to support some government spin doctor programme of big society. In fact we tried to raise awareness of the austerity robbery programme, making people pay for the bankers crisis and illegal wars in other countries.

This was not just a local campaign but a national campaign with ramifications internationally because if a precedent was set of closing down libraries in the UK, this would be repeated in other countries.

169

Libraries provide free education and have helped to raise the level of education in a very significant way in the 19th and 20th centuries. I was told the story of Mr Carnegie, who was apparently a steel multi-millionaire magnet who paid for thousands of libraries across the world. The Carnegie foundation paid a large financial contribution to Friern Barnet Library. The library is owned not by the council, but by the Mayor and Burgesses of Barnet. So some of us question whether the council has the right to sell this building. Apparently Mr Carnegie was not originally a rich man from old money but a poor man who had made good and had begun educating himself from a young age by reading books. He wanted to help others to do the same. There is something very sinister about what the Americans call dumbing down of our education system by the introduction of £9000 university fees and at the same time closing public libraries – beacons of free education, knowledge and learning. In fact we were informed that 250 libraries were to be closed in the UK. One night we sat in the library and did a calculation. If each of those 250 libraries had 8,000 books, as our library had, then that would be over 2,000,000 million books disappearing from circulation. Where were these books going? When the library at Alexandria was burnt down, 2,000,000 scrolls of ancient knowledge disappeared from our world forever, some relating to more advanced pre-flood civilizations. During the discussions online from Guardian readers and others, one lady stated that Waltham Forest council had pulped all the books from their closed-down libraries. During our time at Friern Barnet library we rescued many boxes of books from outside East Finchley library that were left in or around the dustbins. Each box was clearly marked in large red letters, 'dump'. We estimated they were getting rid of 2,000 books. A person of commonsense would assume that these would be redistributed, but this is not always the case. What an incredible waste of knowledge.

While we were at the library we set up the beginnings of a book redistribution, sending multiple copies that we had to Healthy Planet – Free Books for Barnet; a local cancer charity; other squatted social centres; Eritrean refugee camps and to Jamaica. Many of these places were very happy to receive books and we had hoped to continue and expand this service.

Court Cases

We fought two court hearings over the library and were highly successful. Just to explain, I have represented myself for nearly twenty-five years aiming to gain more time for our community projects to be in an empty building, while continuously trying to communicate and negotiate with the owners. All this knowledge was brought to bear in the library case. The aim was always to try and avoid court and agree an interim period where we could use the space until the owner wanted it back. By which time we would move voluntarily without the need of a court order. However, with the library it was a case of hanging on to it until it was returned to the rightful owners, 'the Burgesses of Barnet', the local community. In fact one of the points of our housing campaign is that there should be a register of buildings left empty for over one year and a list or register of people who needed to use them for homes environment/community projects which would in effect create jobs and employment. In fact it is gross government mismanagement of resources to have one and half million buildings sit empty and deteriorating. Some would say this is done to keep us deliberately homeless and to push property prices and rentals falsely inflated.

So it was a slightly bemused judge who cast their eye around 50 assembled people in a packed courthouse that did not have space for another 20-30 people outside. The assembled diversity of squatters, activists, the great and good of Barnet, old and young, the grey rinse revolution, the folk of Barnet and beyond, who were outraged at the council's plan to bulldoze their beloved building and flog it off to the highest bidder. For a supermarket and a block of flats, and forever burying the village green under a large block of concrete. So basically the judge, when I asked for an adjournment to let professional lawyers deal with it, faced with such a throng, granted the adjournment. We rushed outside to jubilant celebrations, and conversations with the media.

The second court case before Judge Pearl, was superbly argued by Sarah Sackman on human rights ground. The case was prepared with the superb skills of Reema Patel, who was legal cavalry to my busy brain, and sterling work by Leigh Day and Co. The judge, although supporting our Human Rights argument, granted a possession order but said that the council to be proportionate must engage in negotiations with the occupiers and the local community to find some sort of solution by January 31st or eviction would take place. *(More information in Reema's chapter)*

REFLECTIONS ON COMMUNITY AND PROTEST

SARAH SACKMAN

For a number of months in the winter of 2011-12, the Occupy protests outside London's St Paul's became a fixture of my route into work and an inescapable mark on the physical and political landscape of this country. The tent city protests reverberated beyond the hundreds, who camped in them, and reflected a widespread disaffection with the global social and economic model which had resulted in a financial crisis and economic downturn. As Richard Sennett has written, more than a critique of capitalism, 'the movement's lasting gift is embodied in the very word "occupy"'. The reclaiming of market squares, city parks and the steps of cathedrals reminded us all of their function as public spaces for political expression and social action.

A year later, I found myself speaking in a packed room at Barnet County Court on behalf of the campaigners to save Friern Barnet Library. The relationship between a campaign to save a local library in a leafy corner of North London, where Margaret Thatcher was once the local MP, and a global protest movement may not seem immediately obvious. However, the campaigners' desire to reclaim an important public space resonated beyond its local setting, demonstrating a grassroots thirst for political agency to bring about real social change.

The Library had been closed and was being prepared to be sold to private developers by Barnet Council notwithstanding powerful local opposition. The handsome red-brick building was boarded up and earmarked for sale; that is until members of London Occupy entered the empty building. In the weeks which followed, local residents donated thousands of books and contributed many man hours to re-open the library. Shelves were filled, book lending resumed and classes from English language to Pilates were arranged. This dynamic campaign was forged from an unlikely coalition of seasoned Occupy activists and Barnet residents, councillors, pensioners, local business people, single mums, young families and religious leaders. It offered a powerful rebuff to the former MP's declaration that "there is no such thing as society".

However, despite the community's welcoming response to the occupation, the Council pressed on with eviction proceedings to get the campaigners out and the estate agents in.

The legal and political strategy

I became involved as the barrister who advised the campaigners on their legal rights and represented them during the eviction proceedings in court. As a barrister you do hundreds of cases, a handful of which capture your imagination. The challenge to save Friern Barnet Library was one of those cases.

When the news of the library protest and re-occupation made the press in September of 2012, the story caught my eye for two reasons. Firstly, because the Library was in Barnet, where I grew up and where my parents used to take me to the local library as a child. Secondly, because the protest was so unusual: instead of the familiar tales of people's impotence in the face of cuts, campaigners had fought back against the library's closure, in the most positive way; by setting up their own community library. It did not take much persuasion for me to take up their case, to work with the campaigners to develop a legal strategy and represent them in court.

Through hours of meetings with the occupiers, local councillors, members of Save Friern Barnet Library and the legal team from Leigh Day & Co, we developed a strategy with the aim of creating the space and the pressure to encourage the Council to negotiate with local people to identify an alternative to closure.

In a community campaign like this, law and politics must go hand in hand. To have any chance of persuading the judge, the Tory-controlled council and the media that the library needed to be saved, it was important to communicate why the library mattered to people. Whilst we would use the legal tools at our disposal to prolong the protest and protect the library, it was necessary that local people did not rely exclusively on litigation. We in the legal team were keen to ensure that the case was a vehicle for empowering members of the campaign and that local people felt able to articulate why the library should be saved without getting bogged down in the jargon and technical aspects of litigation.

There were two aspects to our strategy: Firstly, after Joanna Fryer registered the Library as an asset of community value under the Localism Act 2011, we sent a letter to the council urging the asset to be registered. This reflected the true nature of the library and prevented the Council from selling the Library quickly to a private developer.

And secondly, we argued that the Council's eviction proceedings interfered with the campaigners' freedoms of speech and assembly under Articles 10 and 11 of the Human Rights Act. This changed the nature of the debate shifting the claim from a technical proprietary claim about the eviction of the squatters into what it really was about; a community's protest against the Tory Council's cuts to the Library service.

On 17 December 2012, on a cold Monday morning, it seemed Barnet County Court had become the hottest ticket in town. As I was preparing my notes, I looked up and realised we had packed the court room full with probably a hundred residents. By turning up in such numbers, people demonstrated just how much they cared about the preservation of this cherished public space.

Rejecting the Council's argument, the judge accepted that the campaign to save the library was a legitimate form of protest. She agreed that the occupiers' right of assembly and protest had been engaged but concluded that the Council's interference with those rights in seeking to reclaim the property was proportionate. The court granted the Council possession of the Library, however, critically, the judge delayed the effect of the order by 6 weeks and called on the Council to negotiate with the community.

Eventually, following lengthy negotiations which are documented elsewhere in this book, the Council handed over the keys of the Library to local residents who will now run the library service supported by public funds.

Politics of Place

The campaign's success was based, in part, on people's emotional identification with the Library as a fixture in community life. Libraries everywhere provide access not only to free books and resources but to a social reality outside the market. As Zadie Smith has written, libraries are one of the few institutions where you don't have to buy anything in order to stay.

The campaign epitomised the "politics of place". Public spaces such as libraries, pubs, museums, places of worship and parks, are part of the fabric of the community and a focus for community activism. These shared spaces are cherished precisely because they are public. In an increasingly privatised, atomised world they provide spaces where strangers can come together, notwithstanding their cultural, social and generational differences, and be bound by their commitment to the community.

A library is a social good which matters to people of different political persuasions. It can, as in Barnet, become a focal point for forging new political alliances. On the face of it, the dreadlocked Occupy activists and the smartly-dressed members of SFBL appeared to have little in common. However, the participation in a protest in defence of a vital public space led to collaboration and lasting social ties which challenged prevailing political stereotypes.

Successful campaigns put people first. Fiona Brickwood, one of the campaigners, told me that she had never thought of herself as a political person before the Library campaign. When she took the witness stand in court, she gave an eloquent defence of what the Library meant to local people. Now Fiona, and all those involved in the campaign have been empowered by the experience of community organising to engage in further activism.

The library was saved through the hard work and collective efforts of ordinary people. The months of dedicated protest culminated on 5 February 2013 with Barnet Council handing over the keys of a library it had closed to a group of community individuals.

Today, Friern Barnet Library is open to everyone. Volunteers are running the library in a public building with some resources from the Council and funds raised by the local community (although more are needed). The campaigners rightly insist that they should be supported by public resources and that local government has a legal obligation to provide a library service to its residents.

Given the history of the library, reborn as a result of public protest, it may come as no surprise to readers that Friern Barnet Library continues to serve as a vibrant community hub and forum for political debate - hosting regular classes, lectures, book signings and even political rallies! I am delighted that there is a written record of this inspirational campaign which has reminded us all what grassroots cooperative politics can achieve. I encourage you to visit the Library any day of the week!

AFTERWORD

THERESA MUSGROVE

The contributions in this book vividly capture the feeling of a moment in time, ten years ago now, when a community came together to fight Barnet Council's closure of the much-loved library in Friern Barnet.

We fought, and we won: or so it seemed then. In truth, since that time it has become apparent that we won a battle, but the war had only just begun, and continues even now.

Since the occupation of Friern Barnet Library, and its re-opening as a 'community library', we have been faced with the introduction of cuts in service by the Conservative council on a scale beyond anything we could have imagined.

The idea of a community library, run by volunteers, an outcome that secured the preservation of Friern Barnet branch but abandoned any hope of return to the public service system, has arguably, as many of us feared, provided a template for the council to use when launching a further assault on our libraries, as part of a devastating programme of cuts.

What was once a magnificent 'beacon status' library service is now undergoing a radical deconstruction: some would say a virtual destruction – with half of the library staff losing their jobs, four libraries given to voluntary groups to run, and unstaffed hours in all branches introduced on a massive scale.

This new system is intended to work with the aid of newly installed technology which will give automated entry and self-service to those few residents happy to use a library with no supervision or assistance other than a CCTV camera, monitored from Swansea.

Within the footprint of their own buildings, the library services are being reduced to a fraction of their former space – so as to provide room, we were told, for rentable offices. At the time of writing, there is as yet little evidence of tenants lined up to occupy – if that is the appropriate word – these areas.

The book stock in all libraries has been culled, with boxes of books removed from each branch. Provision for young people and children in need of study space has been drastically reduced.

Outside the libraries undergoing these reductions, and the installation of DIY technology, the council has displayed giant banners, claiming the closures are due to 'refurbishment'.

The most profound impact of these cuts on residents, of course, will be on those most dependent on access to a freely available and professionally staffed public library service - our most vulnerable citizens: the elderly, disabled, disadvantaged residents – and children.

Unaccompanied children under fifteen years old will be barred from the newly unstaffed library hours: an extraordinary restriction that is necessary because of the clear risks presented by the absence of any supervision. Yet other risks are presented for adult users of the new 'open' system – a system that has never been implemented on this scale in a context comparable to Barnet. Obvious risks, from anti-social or even violent behaviour, from drug dealing, from the need to evacuate the premises during a fire: but there are also less obvious consequences, in terms of the impact on residents.

Some of these consequences are indefinable, unpredictable - and immeasurable: how do you assess the social value of a community resource? When elderly residents no longer have a place to go to, within easy reach, where they see familiar faces behind the library counter, and feel less isolated, who will know, or care? When a disabled resident no longer feels they can visit a library that has a difficult automated self-entry system to negotiate, and no one to help them once inside, how will that be recorded, other than as one more statistic in a falling count of visitors?

For children from the less advantaged families in Barnet, the removal of easy access to a library will be quantifiable, perhaps, eventually, as a generation of children in a borough that has always prided itself on a range of exceptional schools, begins to show a decline in achievement and standards of literacy, from primary to secondary level.

For a borough administered by Conservative members still inspired by the legacy of former Finchley MP and PM Margaret Thatcher, this seems an extraordinary rebuttal of the values she held and which they claim to honour: the idea of self-help, and aspiration to something better. For her, access to the public library was central to her early life and education, for the foundation of her career. For her successors in Barnet, it seems, a public library is simply an inconvenience, a public asset, devoid of social value; of material values only, in a future life as an opportunity for development and capital profit.

In one sense, therefore, the story of Friern Barnet library is not what it seemed, at first, the story of triumph over adversity, and the reclamation of a public library. It was the beginning of the end of the public library service as we know it, as we knew it, in this borough.

But there was another victory within that story, and a greater victory, and one which must not be forgotten – and that was the coming together of the community, of friends and allies, and of sections of the community who ordinarily may never have met – a coming together, to unite in a common cause, and to find a strength and sense of power that many had never previously felt was within their grasp.

The real triumph was in that struggle and that victory, and that act of resistance continues to encourage and empower many of those who took part, in ways perhaps they could not have foreseen at the time.

As the newly eviscerated library service begin to re-open in Barnet, and residents begin to see for themselves the reality of 'refurbishment', local campaigners refuse to give in, and continue to fight.

At the beginning of the school holidays this summer, a group of local children went to demonstrate outside the Department of Culture, Media and Sport, and delivered hundreds of letters explaining why they are so angry and upset about the cuts to their local library service.

Watching them stand outside the Department building, with their placards, and then speaking to passers-by about their protest with such passion and articulacy was a deeply inspiring moment.

When a new generation is prepared to stand up and speak out for justice, and the things that matter so much to them, there is hope for the future – even in Broken Barnet, and even when the library door remains firmly shut.

The time of occupation may be over – but the fight continues.

THE END?

ROSIE CANNING

This book has been a long time in the making and since the occupation of Friern Barnet Library in April 2012, many more libraries have been closed, chopped in pieces, or passed on to community groups. According to the *Guardian* in December, 2019: 'Almost 800 libraries have closed since the Conservative -Lib Dem government implemented austerity in 2010, new figures reveal...The number of paid librarians has also plummeted. In 2009/2010, the point marking the start of the Tory-led government's austerity drive, there were 24,000 salaried staff working in libraries. Last year, there were 15,300 employees and more than 51,000 volunteers.'

If there are fewer libraries, then it stands to reason there are fewer books. In Barnet libraries, those that are open, the once packed shelves have been replaced by metal racks that hold fewer books, and this in turn gives the feeling of a hollow emptiness in the libraries as if the axe man cometh at any moment. Over 14,000,000,000 – that's right fourteen million less books are available in British public libraries.

Here in very broken Barnet, it's Groundhog 2018 Election Day again. We've woken up to the same Tory-led council. Libraries are either closed, only open for up to fifteen hours a week or have been handed over to volunteers. And if you're under sixteen and studying, you don't have a hope in hell of using the libraries for research – that's right, under-16s in Barnet are not allowed to use the libraries unless accompanied by an adult! The future is looking very grim.

CONTRIBUTORS

A-Z BIOGRAPHIES

Helene Alderman moved from Islington into Friern Barnet eight years ago attracted, in part, by its library. As a member of the residents' association, she was asked to represent its members in the struggle to keep the building and Library for the community and for posterity.

Tamar Andrusier has lived in Friern Barnet for fifteen years and is proud to have campaigned alongside many dedicated neighbours and friends to save their local public library. Tamar is a musician and teacher and has a strong interest in supporting asylum seekers and refugees. As a professional pianist, Tamar has performed across Europe and broadcast on Radio 3. Tamar enjoys writing songs which have been sung in many of North London's primary schools.

The former London **Borough of Barnet**, now known as Capitaville, is a dystopian corporate state situated on the fringes of North London, run by swivel eyed loon maverick Tories masquerading as elected representatives of their community. This borough has no democracy, no history, and no culture, as they are considered unnecessary, and devoid of marketing potential. In their place we have a people's uprising - 'The Barnet Spring' and a curious phenomenon known as the 'Famous Five' bloggers, who chronicle the downfall of the Conservative administration with loving care and dedication to duty.

Fiona Brickwood has lived in Friern Barnet for many years. In 2011-13, when Barnet Council was requiring the community to find £430,000 to buy the library, she worked with local businesses, councillors, Community Barnet and council officers, trying to develop a business plan to generate the requisite funds and an enterprise to help young people into work. She supported the Occupy group and provided testimony for the court cases. She is now a trustee and volunteer for the Community Library.

Frances Briers has lived in Friern Barnet for twenty-five years. She used the council-run library about twice a week to get books and meet other local people who used the facility. She joined the Save Friern Barnet Library Group to save the last public building left in the area.

All her life **Rosie Canning** has been a book person. As a child, she spent long hours in her local library learning to love books. She grew up in Muswell Hill and went to secondary school near Friern Barnet Library. She worked in an NHS library for thirteen years and is now a PhD Candidate. Rosie co-founded Greenacre Writers, a local writing group and annual literary festival. She's a committed environmentalist and played a key role in getting Friern Barnet Library re-opened.

Dorrell Dressekie wrote the brief history of Friern Barnet Library in 2010, as a project for Friern Barnet and District Local History Society. Dorrel joined the library over 45 years ago when she came to live in Friern Barnet with her children. So, she had good reason to be part of the ongoing campaign to save the library.

Joanna Fryer was born in the USA and got an MA in Classics from the University of Michigan. She came to live and work in Barnet as head of Classics at Finchley Catholic High in 1989. She left to lecture in Classics in the U.S., but prefers life in London, so came back and immediately became involved in saving Friern Barnet Library, of which she is now a trustee.

Mr Greenacres is a passionate and committed environmental campaigner. He often leads walks and gives slide shows. He's a founder member of the Greenacre Project and masterminded the notorious Greenacre Bicycle Rally. He is a master carpenter and musician and is rumoured to have once been a big shot in the music world. Mr Greenacres is the man who re-opened the library.

 Daniel Gardonyi T. was born in Budapest, Hungary and is still alive. He has had many occupations including comedian, video store manager, kitchen slave,, factory worker, squatter, and finally: political activist and peaceful freedom fighter. After 15th October 2011 - Occupy Everywhere Day - he realized he was not alone as a rebel oddball in the world; his life became more meaningful and joyful. So far the most memorable miracle-work on his phantom CV is the Friern Barnet Community Library.

 Barbara Jacobson is Press Officer for the Barnet Alliance for Public Services (BAPS), a coalition of residents, community and campaign groups, and trade unions who want to protect our quality of life, our public services, and our local democracy. BAPS played an active role in the campaign to save Friern Barnet Library and continues to support it.

 Donald Lyven; local resident, taxpayer, watchful consumer, and seasoned curmudgeon. He loves the functional architecture of Friern Barnet library, and it was where he first spoke to his sweetheart Lucy. Once his first novel is published he'll call himself a writer, until then he scrapes a meagre living waving a paintbrush about.

 Theresa Musgrove is the creation of Mrs Angry, who writes the Broken Barnet blog. In an earlier incarnation she worked for Barnet Libraries and was a union convenor. She is a Guardian London top blogger, and a thorn in the flesh of Barnet Council. Eric Pickles thinks she has every right to be angry, and who is going to argue with that?

Lucy Nowell lives in Finchley and works near the Friern Barnet Library. She has been filming and photographing events concerning the library since April 2012. She took photos of possibly the only library open in UK on Christmas Day 2012.

Reema Patel is a trainee lawyer and campaigner who helped the community and the Occupy movement's court case against Barnet Council, in a defence of their rights to protest against the closure of Friern Barnet Library. She advised the trustees on setting up the community group and remains an active community campaigner on a range of local issues.

Maryla Persak-Enefer was born in Poland and qualified as an architect in Warsaw. Since moving to the UK in 1987 she has always lived and worked in the Friern Barnet area. That is also where her children were raised. She has continuously been an active member of the local community and runs her own architectural practice from home. She helped get the local listing for the library.

Phoenix found himself homeless in London at the age of 19. He got into environmental activism through the Twyford Down road protest back in 1992. Over the past twenty-three years, he has continued to set up environment and community centres in some of the million empty buildings in the UK and more recently with the London Occupy Movement. He believes that the empty buildings all around us should be used as community centres, housing and eco project spaces which would create jobs, homes and solutions.

Cllr. Barry Rawlings has been a local Labour councillor (now Leader) since 1998, representing people from both the Friern Barnet and Muswell Hill areas of Barnet. For the last few years, he has worked in safeguarding children with voluntary and faith groups. His firm belief is that politics is relevant and must engage with local community. For him libraries are one of the vital places that help turn a neighbourhood into a community.

In Rwanda, **Alfred Rurangirwa** studied Greek, Latin and modern languages. During the genocide in Rwanda, his family was wiped out along with his home and all his student notes and books. Alfred came to Friern Barnet in 2008 with his five children and joined the library. He was a founding member of SFBLG.

 Martin Russo was a local resident and enjoyed the library services when it was run as a public library. He was a lead campaigner and helped establish Save Friern Barnet Library Group. His main role was as the Communication Officer, and he acted as Chair during the crucial time of the legal case of the Occupy group.

 Sarah Sackman was part of the team that saved Friern Barnet Library and represented the library campaigners in court. Sarah, a graduate of Harvard Law School and Cambridge University practices as a barrister in London specialising in public, planning and environmental law. Her clients include NGOs, local and central government departments and low-income individuals. Sarah has a strong interest in the role of the law in grassroots campaigning.

 Richard Stein is a solicitor and partner at the London law firm Leigh Day. He brings judicial review and other public law cases for claimants only. He has particular expertise in working with public interest groups bringing challenges to decisions of government, quangos, local authorities and the NHS. Recent cases include the Save Lewisham Hospital Campaign case, the AM right to die case, the challenge to the bedroom tax and the UK Uncut challenge to HMRC's handling of Goldman Sachs's tax. He is an experienced campaigner and was once a local councillor.

 Roger Tichborne is a dyslexic punk rock guitarist, studio owner and author of Barnet Eye blog. Born and raised in the London Borough of Barnet. Loves beer, curry and football and occasionally strings two coherent sentences together. He launched the Save Barnet's Libraries Campaign in August 2010 and then the Friern Barnet Peoples Library pop up Library in April 2012.

Donnie Vortex left university in 2011 in search of truth, and to help with the suffering of the world. His main influences are the teachings of the Buddha, the works of George Orwell, and the example of non-violent civil disobedience set by Mahatma Gandhi. It was love at first sight with Friern Barnet Library; he spent long hours leafing through her many pages. He misses her dearly but is glad she's happy.

ACKNOWLEDGEMENTS

THANK YOU FOR THOSE DAYS

To members of the Occupy Movement not in the book without who there would not be a library or a community building, including: Arun Mistry, Leon Pike, Petra Rakocz, Hymn, Raffe, Tiffany, Thor, Tammy, Stefan and Pedro Lima.

38degrees for running the petition to re-open the library. Thanks to Richard Reeve who suggested Leigh Day (thanks to them too) and Ugo Hayter who worked tirelessly in the background. Ollie Natelson and Dorrell Dressekie who contributed to the contents of the local listing application document. Also, those people who supported the Listing application Clare Wright, Alicja Szmelter, Ela Miszta-Golebiewska, Anne Levens, Audrey Fairclough, Alison Hunt, and especially to: The Twentieth Century Society; The Society for the Protection of Ancient Buildings; Andrew Dismore; Friern Barnet and Whetstone Residents' Association; and Friern Village Residents' Association.

Huge thanks to all the members of the Save Friern Barnet Library Group and those not mentioned in the book including Ben, Fiona Cockrane, Sheri Darby, Paul Merchant, Sarah Howe. Thanks to the Royal British Legion, whose unwavering support gave many a weary traveller a place to rest. Thanks also to Samar Barakat, Cllr. Pauline Oakley-Webb, Rosa De Souza and anyone else who helped save the library. And lastly to all the contributors of this book who gave their writing.

With thanks to the following for the use of material:
Friern Barnet and District Local History Society

Printed in Great Britain
by Amazon

85318093R00108